CATCHING SALMON

Richard Waddington

D0506733

DAVID & CHARLES
NEWTON ABBOT   LONDON   NORTH POMFRET (VT)   VANCOUVER

British Library Cataloguing in Publication Data

Waddington, Richard
Catching salmon
1. Salmon-fishing
I. Title

799.1'7'55   SH684

ISBN 0–7153–7533–4

Library of Congress Catalog Card Number 77–85034

© Richard Waddington 1978

Set by Trade Linotype Limited
and printed in Great Britain by
Redwood Burn Limited, Trowbridge and Esher
for David & Charles (Publishers) Limited
Brunel House   Newton Abbot   Devon

Published in the United States of America
by David & Charles Inc
North Pomfret   Vermont 05053   USA

Published in Canada
by Douglas David & Charles Limited
1875 Welch Street   North Vancouver   BC

Contents

1	Why Does the Salmon Take?	7
2	Factors Influencing the Salmon's Behaviour	13
3	Practical Applications of the Theory—Fly-Fishing	42
4	Fishing the Sunk Fly—Strategy	53
5	Greased-Line Fishing	72
6	Presentation	80
7	Fishing the Fly	90
8	Bait-Fishing	106
9	Spinning for Salmon	109
10	Spinning in Summer	117
11	Prawn and Shrimp	123
12	Fishing the Worm	131
13	Dry-Fly Fishing and Float-Fishing	142
14	Fair Fishing	149
	Index	155

1

Why Does the Salmon Take?

Fishing has one quality which makes it unique among sports. The shooting man with gun and dog hunts his unwilling prey and kills it. The foxhunter chooses an even more unwilling quarry for his hounds to kill. The stalker creeps up on an unsuspecting animal and shoots it down. The fisherman does none of these things. For indeed in fishing it is the angler that is the hunted. Playing innocently with his fly or bait he finds it seized by a rapacious creature whose one thought is to steal it from him. The roles are reversed. The fish is the hunter, the angler is the hunted.

Fishing, then, if it is to be undertaken in a rational manner, demands a different mental approach from that required by other sports. To be successful the fisherman must project his mind into the very strange world which the fish inhabits. He must try to imagine what the fish is doing, how his little fishy mind is thinking, how a weightless cold-blooded creature reacts to his environment, what makes him hungry, or makes him fast; why at one moment does he seem asleep, and at another very actively awake.

The sea angler, the coarse fish angler and the trout fisherman are clear about one thing. The fish that takes their proffered bait does so because it wants to eat. The singular charm of salmon fishing lies in the fact that the salmon neither

7

wishes to eat nor could do so even if it wished!

Because so much of the pleasure in salmon fishing lies in thinking intelligently about one's actions, in trying to understand those of the fish and in marrying the techniques of the one to the reactions of the other, much of the early part of this book is devoted to an examination of the fish and his environment. Fishing for salmon is often regarded as a 'chuck and chance it' form of angling by the dry fly trout purist. In fact, the successful salmon fisherman requires more knowledge, more finesse, better techniques and imaginative approach than is ever needed in presenting an imitation of a fly on which a trout can be seen to be feeding.

The fundamental problem confronting the fisherman is that of providing a reasonable answer to the question, 'Why does the salmon take a fly or bait?'. Until he can satisfy himself on this point he is never in a position to fish intelligently. A number of explanations have been given at various times, most of which range from the faintly to the sublimely ridiculous.

Let us glance cursorily at some of the more reasonable of these explanations and see why they must be rejected. The oldest and most obvious is that the salmon takes the fly because he is hungry. This theory suffered an early eclipse when it was noted that the stomachs of fish taken in the river or the estuaries were, in all save the most exceptional cases, entirely devoid of food. It was then propounded that the fish did not eat in fresh water because his stomach and digestive processes had atrophied and the conclusion was correctly drawn that the salmon did not take on account of hunger. We shall re-examine this question later. For the moment it is sufficient to note that, whereas the conclusion is almost certainly correct, the reasoning leading to it is open to grave doubts. The unfortunate result of this conclusion, however, was that the one and only explanation that gave the fish a conscious choice in whether he took or not was foundered.

Why Does the Salmon Take?

To replace the now defunct theory of hunger we have been offered at various times propositions based upon fear, anger, curiosity, reflex action, instinct and amusement. All of them have certain points in their favour, but none of them individually or collectively can satisfy us. There are three main questions upon which any answer to the problem must satisfy us. Firstly, why does this fish take such monstrosities as flies and lures? Secondly, why are his demands as to sizes at different times of year so specific? Thirdly, why, at one moment, does he allow an easy prey to pass unmolested well within his reach while, at another, he sets upon it with avidity?

Fear as a reason comes off very badly when examined critically. It answers the first of our questions, but none of the others. It suffers, too, from the overwhelming weakness that the salmon is a fish possessing no defensive or offensive armament, despite the remarkable picture opposite p112 in Mr Wandless' *Angler's Creel*, which purports to be the jaw of a monster Loch Awe salmon, but which might well be the jaw of Walt Disney's Big Bad Wolf. However, this is true only of the salmon in fresh water. The pelagic salmon is armed with a formidable array of teeth which fall out at the beginning of his migration back to the river. A new set of teeth certainly begins to grow while in fresh water and the autumn fish and the kelt are about as well equipped, comparatively, as a trout. But these freshwater teeth never achieve the size of those which Dr Tchernavin has noted in his study of the dentition of immature salmon (I believe *Onchorynchus*, the Pacific Salmon, and not *Sulur*). The natural reaction of the salmon to fear is flight. Nevertheless it may well be, as we shall see later, that fear, or rather fright, may at times have a secondary effect in disturbing fish and causing an erstwhile non-taker to become, later, a taking fish.

Anger fares rather better under examination. I am aware that in that magnificent compendium on the sport in The

Why Does the Salmon Take?

Lonsdale Library, Mr Eric Taverner turns down somewhat brusquely the suggestion that salmon take because of 'the desire to seize, kill, or destroy anything that annoys them'. He presents his reader with the picture of an angry fish wandering about a pool sullenly seeking a victim and, finding none, returning to his lie to 'await a state of peace with the world'. While wholeheartedly agreeing with Mr Taverner that anger is not the reason, I cannot but admit that in presenting his argument in the manner of *reductio ad absurdum* he has failed to make his point. The protagonist of the anger school argues, very reasonably, that it is not any bad temper, attack of liver, or whim inherent in the fish that provides an attack, but that it is the proximity of the fly that enrages the fish. I have several times experienced definite cases where a fish has, to all appearances, been taunted into taking by repeated casting of the fly over his nose. Were it not for the fact that one may ascribe this phenomenon rather to the general disturbance of the fish's environment, which has reduced him to becoming a taker, than to active fury, it would be difficult for any angler to discard what is, after all, the evidence of his own eyes.

Unfortunately the anger theory must be discarded as ruthlessly as any other that fails to answer all our three questions. Why does the presence of the lure not always have this effect? Why is the angry fish not far more catholic in his choice of victims? Why, in a pool containing perhaps many hundreds of fish, should only one or two exhibit these signs of bad temper? No. It does not hold water and it must go.

The same objections hold good for curiosity as a motive. Fish are undoubtedly curious at moments about baits and flies moving within their range of vision. They sometimes follow them for quite long distances before either taking or turning away from them. But again we must ascribe to curiosity only a secondary effect. I do not think it is curiosity that makes the fish interested. It is something else that rouses

10

him in the first place. Can that something else be the flash of the tinsel on the fly or from the side of the spinning bait? It has been suggested that this flash causes a reflex reaction in the fish which, rather as a baby automatically puts out its hand to grasp the shining watch dangled in front of it, seizes the fly because it cannot help itself.

If this were true, how easy would the fisherman's lot become. No more doubts, no more trial and error, no more blank days—he would merely put on a flashing bait every time he wanted to catch a fish. Obviously this is not the reason. Flashing in some degree or another is associated with every creature that swims in sea or river, and there is little doubt but that the bright parts of the successful lure serve to heighten the illusion that it is a living creature.

Another argument of the same type is that which supposes that the bait represents a small creature in difficulties or injured and that it is instinctive for the salmon to attack such an easy prey. We are told that this instinct is common to all the predators and may extend, as for instance in the case of wolves, even to devouring members of their own pack who fall by the wayside. Here again we have a proposition that fails to pass the test of our three queries. But we have now run up against a word—instinct—which, unless we are very careful, is going to be a stumbling block to the seeker after the truth all along the road.

This word, meaning according to the *Oxford Dictionary* 'innate propensity, especially in lower animals, to certain seemingly rational acts performed without conscious design', is really only the zoologist's jargon for saying, 'I am not able to give any other explanation so I call it instinct'. You will find that wherever any behaviour or movement of a bird or animal cannot be explained in simple terms, instinct is held responsible. Because, for instance, we are not yet quite sure how a pigeon finds his way back to his own loft, we state that the homing instinct guides him. A dog, however,

11

which has usually this ability of finding his way home very strongly developed is not normally said to possess this homing instinct. Why not? Simply because we can very easily see that the dog is using either his sense of vision or his sense of smell to find his way. There ceases to be any mystery and there is no need to invoke instinct. In salmon fishing there is a tendency to invoke instinct at every turn.

Those who have read William Scrope's classic, *Days and Nights of Salmon Fishing in the Tweed*, will remember how, with his tongue in his cheek, this author suggests that the fish takes the fly merely for the sake of passing the time and amusing himself. Scrope, of course, never intended that this suggestion should be taken seriously—and yet it is the one which comes nearest of all to providing an answer to the three queries which we have said must be satisfied before any explanation to the main problem, 'Why does the salmon take?', can be accepted. To the first of our queries 'Why such monstrosities as flies and lures?' the answer 'Amusement' is quite satisfactory. To the third, 'Why at one moment does he take and not at another?' the same answer will do. Like the Great Queen, the salmon has moments when he is 'not amused'. But alas, Scrope's suggestion fails at the second query, 'Why are his demands as to sizes at different times of the year so specific?'. And so, regretfully, we must rule this theory out of court also.

We have so far failed to find any answer, or for that matter, any combination of answers, that will satisfy us. The answers rule out some of the more plausible theories generally put forward and we have not yet succeeded in replacing them with anything more reasonable. We have, too, shelved for the moment the possibility that it is hunger that drives the salmon to take the fly. Let us examine what evidence we have about the habits of this fish and see what we are able to deduce from it.

12

2

Factors Influencing the Salmon's Behaviour

We know a lot more about the life history and the migration of the salmon today than we did twenty years ago. The blank chapter of his sea life is now largely written in. We know, at least in general terms, where the migrating smolt goes to, where he remains feeding, and quite a lot about what he feeds on.

Unfortunately this recently acquired knowledge has done much to endanger the survival of the salmon as a species. Already netted and trapped to excess off the coast and in the river itself, the discovery of the salmon feeding grounds in the North Atlantic enabled drift netting by sea-going trawlers to take fish, mature and immature, in frightening quantities in the Denmark Strait and off the Greenland coast. Happily the danger to the salmon has been recognized and much of this pelagic netting has been stopped under international agreement.

The salmon at sea, with his newly grown, very formidable array of teeth, feeds largely on herring and capelin. He also takes various type of prawn or krill and, at certain seasons, loligo—a form of small squid or octopus. And we know, from reading his scales—which, like trees, are marked with growth rings—that for part of the year he feeds more avidly than at other times; and we conclude that the periods of heavier

feeding correspond perhaps with the shoaling of herring or capelin, and of lighter feeding with the breaking up of these shoals and the necessity of hunting perhaps the loligo or crustaceans. The scale markings give a clear picture of a seasonal abundance of food followed by a leaner period.

The important point about the scale evidence for the angler is that it tends to indicate that there is a duality about the salmon's life in the ocean—one period during which he feeds exceedingly well, another during which he finds food more difficult to acquire, or possibly during which he lives on some entirely different food.

When we observe the behaviour of the fish in fresh water we are at first rather surprised to discover that there is also a duality about his life here. Every fisherman knows that during the early spring the salmon takes a large fly sunk deep and that during the summer he takes a small fly fished very near the surface of the water and that, further, each method of fishing is, with few exceptions, successful only during its own season of the year. It seems that there must be some connection between his marine and his freshwater behaviour.

Should we regard the salmon as a sea or a freshwater fish? The point at first appears academic, but, again, it is of certain interest to the practical angler.

Though I know that there is a school that holds the opposite view, I must state it is my belief that the salmon is a freshwater fish that is at present undergoing a rather rapid evolutionary change. *Salmo salar*, the salmon, belongs to the genus *Salmo* which embraces the trouts (*S. trutta* or *S. fario*) the Rainbow (*S. irideus*) and several sub-species all of which, with the exception of the sea trout and the slob or estuarine trout, are unquestionably freshwater fish entirely. These are, as it were, the salmon's first cousins. More distantly related are the remainder of the family of Salmonidae of which the

Summer evening on the Dee (*Wildlife Services*)

other members found in Britain are the Char and the Fontinalis. The family, incidentally, has as its characteristic the adipose, or second dorsal fin, which is unique in that it is not supported by a rib.

While we may be in doubt about the salmon, the sea trout and that large class of intermediate estuarine fish, the whole genus *Salmo* share one important common feature which, to my mind, conclusively stamps them as of freshwater origin. Any who indulge in pelagic wanderings must return to fresh water to breed. That illustrious biologist, the late Professor J. Arthur Thomson, under whom I was privileged to study, wrote this much-quoted passage: 'When an animal has two different haunts THE SPAWNING GROUND OR REPRODUCTIVE AREA INDICATES THE ORIGINAL HOME. Flounders may be caught many miles up-river, but they go down to the salt water to spawn; the sea snakes may be seen swimming a hundred miles from land, but they reproduce among the shore rocks; the robber crab climbs the coco plants, but it has to go back to the shore to breed, and so on through a long list.'

The race of any of this family will not survive unless access can be had to fresh water for the rearing of the young. On the other hand, there are several lakes in which salmon have become landlocked and in which they have managed to survive as a species without ever going to the sea. Biologically, then, we must regard the salmon as a freshwater fish that has taken to the sea for better feeding and quicker growth.

The angler, of course, is not really interested in the biological niceties of this question. But, as we shall see, when we have examined our final piece of evidence, the angler is vitally interested in the fact that the fish has taken to the sea for better feeding and quicker growth.

This final piece of evidence refers to a question which we shelved earlier on in Chapter 1, namely 'Does the salmon take a fly or bait because he is hungry?'. In other words, does he eat or desire to eat in fresh water? Controversy over this

16

question has raged with unabated fury for more than half a century, and because every angler has been encouraged to hold his own individual views regardless of the factual evidence, disagreement on this matter has flourished even to the extent of breaking up lifelong friendships.

There are many die-hards who maintain that the salmon feeds in fresh water. Fortunately, however, most fishermen are reasonable creatures and have come to accept as fact the view that salmon do not eat in fresh water. The point at issue is nowadays rather a smaller one, namely, 'Can the salmon eat in fresh water if he wants to?'.

In giving an answer to this we are on fairly sure ground. The salmon does not eat in fresh water because he cannot; and he cannot because his digestive processes have, to a certain extent, atrophied. (Atrophy, from the Greek a = not, trophe = food means 'wasting away through imperfect nourishment'. It does not mean 'destroyed'.)

This fish starts to fast while still in the sea and well away from the coast. All save a very few of the fish that are taken in the coast nets are already well into their fast and there are grounds for supposing that it is started while the fish is still in his feeding places. Indeed, some authorities hold that the reason that the fish leaves his marine haunt is because he has reached a state of satiety. More probably, however, is the supposition that it is the beginnings of the maturing of the sexual glands which sends the fish off on his journey and that, on becoming a traveller, he eschews the pleasures of feeding.

Though the fish undoubtedly fasts from some date prior to his arrival off the coast until, perhaps some fifteen months later, he (or more probably, she) reaches the sea again, the stomach does not undergo any organic transformation which renders it incapable of functioning. It does, however, atrophy through disuse. The gut contracts and ceases to secrete the digestive juices. The liver ceases to function. We have a parallel in a minor way, in the human race. Something of the same sort occurs to a man who has undergone a long period of starvation. And just as such a man is quite incapable of dealing with a normal meal because his stomach has partly atrophied, so it is impossible for the fish to feed in the normal way. Moreover, it is probable that the fish is quite incapable of experiencing the sensation of hunger.

Nevertheless, there are several well authenticated cases of salmon having passed small fish such as roach or dace into the stomach. There is also the phenomenon witnessed by most experienced anglers of large numbers of fish rising to the surface of a pool and quite definitely taking flies floating on the water exactly in the manner of trout. I have taken the trouble, when fishing the worm, to examine the stomachs of many salmon and sea trout. I have never yet found a fish which, though given plenty of time to chew the bait, has passed any part of it into the stomach. Almost invariably I have found that pieces of worms can be seen lodged in the gill clefts indicating that the chewed, and perhaps tasted, food is passed out through the gills. It is quite possible that the average salmon may swallow a totally unsuspected quantity of food during his sojourn in the river. But he can derive no nourishment from it; he does not take it because he is hungry; he is not, in fact, feeding.

Why then does the salmon take a fly? We have had many hints as to the probable reason in this short review of his marine life. We have found the probability of a duality in his method of life in the sea; and, strangely enough, we have observed this duality also in his behaviour in the river. We have seen that the salmon is almost certainly a freshwater fish when judged biologically, but a fish that has taken up a sea habit of feeding. And we have also seen that, though the salmon does not feed in fresh water and cannot do so, nevertheless he sometimes, if not often, has been known to take food into his mouth and pass it into the stomach.

From all this and from observation of the fish's behaviour in the river we are able to postulate a theory which accounts for many of the mysteries surrounding the sport of salmon fishing. We will suppose that the duality that we have suspected in the fish's marine life arises from the fact that, for a part of the year, he lives in deeper water feeding on a well stocked but not overflowing larder. At some date, probably in the late spring, either a warm current sweeps over his feeding beds, or possibly the fish moves into other waters where an abundance of food exists, and he remains here feasting and resting until winter comes.

I believe that this duality is reflected in the salmon's river life. Further, I believe that it is because he has the habit of hunting and seizing his food so strongly ingrained upon his nature that, under certain conditions which we shall examine later, he is unable to resist the habit of hunting even in the very different surroundings of the river, and it is this that causes him to take the fly. It is force of habit and not fear, anger, instinct or curiosity that accounts for the one weakness that allows him to fall prey to the angler.

Under normal circumstances, the memory of his hunting days are forgotten by the salmon in the very different surroundings of the river; but certain stimuli, certain changes in his environment may reawaken the remembrance of his sea life, and for a few moments, a few hours perhaps, he becomes once again Nimrod or Bahram.

I do not claim that this theory is new or revolutionary. It is not; but hitherto the possibility that it may be the force of a lifetime's habit of feeding and hunting that is the motive for the salmon taking has been regarded as very remote.

DUALITY OF LIFE IN SEA/RIVER

It is my intention in this book to show that if we start off with the assumption that, from the angler's point of view and in direct contradiction to the biological facts, the salmon is

19

a sea fish and retains at moments his sea behaviour when in the river, and that if we build up a theory upon this premise and push it to its logical conclusions, we shall find ourselves with a simple and satisfactory explanation for every angle of the behaviour of our fish when in the river. We shall, too, have removed much of the mumbo-jumbo and the mystery from the sport and I hope that this theory will help the reader, as it has done the writer, very materially to increase his catches.

The fisherman who can go down to the river quite certain of which fly or bait to use and of the way to fish it on any day of the year is at an enormous advantage over his fellows. Most anglers fail both in material success and in securing the maximum of pleasure from the sport through being unable to give themselves a logical explanation for their actions. Not only does this result in uncertainty and trial and error methods of fishing, but in a tremendous waste of time.

Having decided that it is to the habits formed by the salmon in the sea that we must ascribe the peculiarities of his river life, and that he takes a lure because, for the time being at any rate, some stimulus has reawakened the remembrance of his hunting days, the next point to consider is the anomaly of his fastidiousness over the size and method of presentation of the lure he is prepared to take at the various seasons. Why, in February, will he seize a 4in Ackroyd or a large spratt fished several feet below the surface and in May a No 6 Blue Charm fished almost on the surface—and why will he not look at the same Ackroyd or spratt in May and ignore the No 6 fly in February?

The answer to this lies in the duality of his sea life. Because of the fact that the salmon is so very definitely fastidious over the size of bait he will take, it must be concluded that he is mistaking it for some creature of which he has full cognizance and which he has been in the habit of hunting under similar conditions of light, temperature, length of day

20

or other comparable circumstances. I do not for one moment believe that it is merely fortuitous that particular sizes of flies, for instance, are successful. I am going to suggest, therefore, that during the winter and early spring the salmon lives in fairly deep waters off the Continental Shelf, and that during this period he feeds mainly off smaller fish of the herring and capelin families and also, when he can find it, a small squid or cuttlefish of about the same size. I suggest that these staple foods of the salmon exist, not in the very deep waters, but in a layer of water certainly not on the surface.

When the spring arrives, probably in April, a warm current, the North Atlantic Drift, sweeps over these feeding grounds of the salmon, bringing with it a new and very plentiful supply of food. This, I suggest, is some small, thin, tenuous fish of little more than 1in in length which inhabits the topmost surface layers of the ocean current which carries it. I have suggested that this may well be the *Leptocephalus*, or immature elver, which makes its way in prodigious quantities and in an endless stream from its birthplace in the Sargasso Sea to the European coast and takes no less than three years over the journey. When a comparison is made between the life histories, range, habit, and abode of the Atlantic salmon and the European eel, we shall see later that there is a very strong case to be made out for the hypothesis that much of the salmon's existence is bound up with that of the eel. Equally, however, it may be that the salmon now feeds on the small shrimps, the krill, which abound in such quantities where the cold polar currents meet the warm waters of the Gulf Stream that they enable the whalebone whales to grow into some of the largest creatures on earth.

The point, for the moment, is that the salmon's sea life shows a duality of existence and feeding that is reflected in the river behaviour of the fish and that, because there is no gradual transition period from one type of sea feeding to another but a sudden break caused by the advent, possibly, of a stream of warm water, the angler must be prepared to regard the salmon in cold and in warm water either as two entirely different species of fish or as one species having two different phases of existence. There is no transition period between the winter and summer feeding. The scale readings show this quite clearly; but it seems probable by the same token that the summer feeding gradually falls off and merges into winter feeding. Of this we shall see more later. Similarly, in the river, it is no gradual transition to which our fishing methods must conform. The change from spring fishing to summer fishing is sudden and dramatic. For spring fishing in cold water we use the large fly fished deep or a large bait, for summer fish in warm water we use the small fly and the greased-line or a tiny spinner. There is no half-way house and no bastard method that can at any time be successful. When we come to examine the structure of the salmon's eye and to discuss what he sees, we shall find that these two types of bait represent to the fish a fairly accurate picture of what he would expect to see and hunt in one or other of his periods of ocean life.

We shall see, too, how important the surface of the water is to the angler in the summer, and how negatively important it is in the winter and spring. We shall understand also the fact that bait-fishing has often proved more successful than the fly during the spring. And when we have finished putting together the two and two of what we know as facts and what we can conjecture from them, we shall have a fairly complete answer to the questions 'Why does the salmon take a fly?', and 'WHEN, WHERE and HOW does the salmon take?'.

Having established that it is habit that causes the salmon to take, the next problem that confronts the angler is to discover why it is only at certain times that this habit predominates, and if possible to ascertain what physical or other factors affect the fish at these times and why the fish reacts to them in this manner.

22

The Laxford at Laxford Bridge. The word lax is the Norse word for salmon, and this river, together with Loch Stack from which it flows is one of the best of the west coast of Scotland salmon rivers. For its length it is certainly the most prolific sea trout river in Scotland. Short, mostly tidal, this is a typical west coast spate river—wonderfully good when there is water, woefully bad when the river is low (*L. S. Paterson*)

Factors Influencing the Salmon's Behaviour

We may presume that while in the sea the salmon, always a voracious feeder, seizes his prey whenever opportunity presents itself and that it is only when he is temporarily sated that he will rest from pursuit of his quarry. It is possible that tidal influences may have some effect upon his feeding habits, and it seems probable that he is not able to hunt as successfully during the hours of darkness as during the daytime. But in general, we must regard any creature that grows as fast as the salmon in the sea as feeding almost incessantly. And we cannot, therefore, attribute the choice of times when the fish is prepared to take in the river to any habit of feeding at certain times only in the sea. We must look, then, to some physical factors in his new environment, the river itself, to provide the answer.

FRESH WATER

When considering the different conditions which salmon encounter in fresh water the first thing that we must remember is that it is not due to any effect of the river that the fish stops feeding. This phenomenon occurs while he is still far out at sea and, probably, while still on his feeding grounds. And it is during his journey to the coast that his digestive processes atrophy and the fish starts his fast. Before the influence of fresh water is ever felt, the salmon has already given up hunting for food. And it is for this reason that, while they may sometimes be seen in large numbers in the sea off some of our west-coast rivers waiting for water to run them, unlike the sea trout which often take readily in salt water, instances of salmon being caught on rod and line in the sea are virtually unknown.

On entering fresh water, the salmon encounters a medium obviously very different from that in which he has lived for the past year or two. Yet, curiously enough, the change that at first appears the most profound is accomplished with an ease and despatch that is quite remarkable, and with no

24

detectable physical adjustment in the fish himself. I refer to the change from salt to fresh water. The salmon taken in the sea nets and his brother taken shortly after he has entered a river pool are identical. It is only by examining the parasite sea lice that both carry that the one may be distinguished from the other. Nor is there, when conditions for entering the river are right, any hesitation or any necessity for a gradual acclimatization on the part of the fish. Just as the netting experiments in the Norwegian fiords and, earlier, in the Tay estuary have shown that the smolt, as soon as he hits the tidal water, runs straight out to sea, so does the incoming salmon, once he reaches the mouth of the river, run straight up into the freshwater pools.

When we consider that there is a large class of Euryhaline fish (the shads, sturgeon, even the estuarine trout are examples) which lives and feeds quite at random in either salt, brackish or fresh water, I do not think we should be really surprised that the salmon is able to accomplish this changeover with such facility. Yet there are enormous problems to be overcome. For instance, the specific gravity of salt and fresh water are different and the fish must make an adjustment in his balance on changing from one to the other. Likewise the salinity of the sea is greater than that of his body fluids, of fresh water lower than that of his blood or cell contents. In the sea the fish has to replace fluid lost through osmosis, in fresh water he has to excrete excess fluid to prevent himself becoming waterlogged. That his renal system is designed to cope with such fundamental problems is nothing short of miraculous; that on returning once again to fresh water it cannot, at one and the same time, deal with the waste products of the fish's metabolism and with those of feeding is not surprising. The priority in the returning salmon is the next generation. The disposal of the waste products engendered by the changes in the fish's body tissue as the reproductive cells grow cannot ever be successfully accomplished; and the fact

25

that his renal system could never deal with the additional strain imposed by feeding is almost certainly the reason that salmon cannot and do not feed while in fresh water.

It is, then, to the influence of some factor or factors peculiar to the river that we must look for an explanation of the salmon's behaviour in fresh water. Salinity apart, there is one other major difference between sea water and fresh water. In the sea, conditions tend to remain virtually static. In the river they are infinitely variable; the temperature is variable, the volume of water, and the speed of the current is variable, the acidity is variable, and, above all, the amount of oxygen dissolved in the water and upon which the fish depends for his very life is variable. These variations are not gradual fluctuations that occur with the changing seasons but are daily and often hourly variations. And it is to this instability in the medium in which he now finds himself that the peculiarities of the behaviour of the salmon in fresh water can be entirely attributed.

In attempting to analyse the reaction of the fish to these variations—an attempt that must be made if we are to arrive at the truth—we come up against a serious obstacle. It is not possible to describe accurately a fish's feeling in human terms, for no man can even conceive the conditions of life in the fish's world. Our vision, for instance, is limited only by a horizon which recedes as we gain altitude. The fish, on the other hand, can see but dimly through the surface of the water in an arc of less than 90° directly above him. The remainder of the surface acts as a mirror and reflects only the bottom of the stream. The fish breathes in a different manner, hears differently, has an almost non-existent sense of touch except near the median line of his body, and is sensitive to heat and cold in a totally different way from a warm-blooded creature.

In discussing the effects of variations in temperature upon the salmon this difficulty is at once apparent. As warm-blooded animals we are more sensitive to variations in temperature, especially when accompanied by changes in the humidity of the air, than to any other atmospheric phenomenon. And because it is no uncommon thing to experience a daily variation of air temperature of 40°–50°F our comfort and sense of well-being is largely dependent upon the thermometer. But while air temperatures may vary enormously in twenty-four hours, during the same period the water temperature will vary by little more than a degree or two, and because the fish always maintains his own bodily temperature slightly above that of the water his reaction to this very gradual change is merely to allow his own temperature to rise and fall in conformity. Within limits, the salmon is never able to determine whether it is warm or cold, and while he is certainly aware of any change in temperature, he is subjected to none of the violent reflex reactions undergone by a man walking out of a warm room into the open air on a frosty morning; and as soon as his bodily adjustment to the change is completed all sensation of warmth or cold must disappear.

Nevertheless, for want of any better explanation, it has been to his reactions to temperature that the peculiarities of the salmon's behaviour in fresh water have generally been attributed. And while I have no doubt that, indirectly, temperature has a profound influence upon his habits, such evidence of its direct influence upon the fish, save at one critical point, all goes to show that temperature as an individual factor has little, if any, effect upon the fish's actions. Calderwood has shown that the temperature of the water has no effect upon the date of the entry of fish into any particular river. Attempts have often been made to provide, on the grounds of temperature alone, an explanation for the fact that some rivers are spring rivers and others late summer rivers. These have always failed because, invariably, several exceptions, for which no logical explanation could be given, have been found. There is no observable difference in the willingness of salmon to take in a cold February, when the river is only just off freezing, than in a February when the water is well over 40°F. That salmon will neither enter the river nor run in snow water has been observed and noted by every Scottish fisherman, and the temptation to ascribe this entirely to the coldness of the water has been too strong even for such experts as W. J. M. Menzies. Mr Menzies, however, realising that in ascribing the speed and distances covered by running fish to temperature alone he was facing many inexplicable anomalies, has qualified this by adding the influence of the 'nature of the bed of the river'. In other words, he says that in cold *and fast* water fish will not run, while they may do so in cold *and slow* water. This is observably a correct statement of fact, and fits in well with the theory that it is the rising temperature that induces the fish to move higher and higher up the river as the season progresses. But the one fact that destroys the probability of the truth in this theory is the behaviour of the fish in September and October. By now the river is beginning to cool, and accordingly the fish should stop running. In fact, of course, they run at this period of the year probably faster and further than at any other time.

I think that in combining the explanations of the temperature and the nature of the bed of the river Mr Menzies has approached very near to the truth without quite attaining it. Both of these factors are responsible for the behaviour, particularly as regards entering the river and running, but not directly responsible. It is through their effect upon the oxygen content of the river water that they chiefly influence the salmon. It can be shown, as conclusively as circumstantial evidence will ever permit, that it is the oxygen content, the amount of free oxygen dissolved in the river water, that is the controlling factor in the salmon's behaviour from the moment he approaches the river mouth until spawning is completed. The only reason, in fact, that the salmon ever returns to fresh water is because, though fully emancipated from river life as a mature fish, he is not yet acclimatized sufficiently as a species to be able to breed in the sea. And the reason that his eggs will not hatch and his young are unable to exist in the alevin stage in the sea is not, as might be supposed, initially on account of its salinity, but almost certainly because the oxygen content of sea water is not high enough. It is also a fact that the specific gravity of the salmon's eggs is too low for hatching in the sea. If placed in sea water they float.

This statement is going to meet with much opposition and, therefore, cannot stand as it is without elaboration. It is a curious fact that, in spite of many years of hatchery practice and experiment, no one has yet laid down the minimum amount of dissolved oxygen required in water for the successful hatching and rearing of salmon and trout. And yet here we have the strange phenomenon of all the members of the genus *Salmo* exhibiting the same urge to get to the headwaters of the stream in which they live, some of them all their lives, others of them for part of their lives only, for the purpose of reproducing their species. There must be some good reason for it, for nature does not ordain a course of action for her creatures without cause. We may hazard that perhaps altitude or air pressure may be responsible; that possibly it is temperature or the type of plant life found in the headwaters that influences the fish's choice. But when we consider that the range of salmon and trout in Britain alone is in waters of an infinity of temperature, altitudes, acidity, plant life, and almost every other variable factor, we are driven to look for something outside this as the motivating influence.

OXYGEN

When, however, we examine the habitat of salmon and trout we find that they are unable, apparently, to exist in water containing less than about 6cc of dissolved oxygen per litre, though carp, for instance, are able to live, but not to breed, in water with about 3cc. Moreover, we find that when confined to water of between 6cc and 7cc of dissolved oxygen content trout, at any event, are incapable of breeding at all, and that unless the water contains over 7cc any eggs that are laid either do not hatch or do not produce offspring that live beyond the yolk-sac stage. We are justified in concluding that, other factors being suitable, it is the amount of dissolved oxygen in the water that will determine whether salmon and trout can reproduce their species in any given stream; and it can be shown that it is invariably the headwaters of all rivers that are not only highly oxygenated, but remain so throughout the year and do not suffer from the diurnal variations occasioned by the growth of weed and algae found in the lower reaches.

Even more than the trout is the salmon dependent upon a high oxygen content for the successful hatching and rearing of his young. The maturing fish is so constructed by nature that, as the season advances and the sexual characteristics ripen, so do the physical needs for a higher concentration of oxygen in his medium increase. Because the word instinct is so unsatisfactory it is impossible to dismiss the urge of the salmon to get into sufficiently highly oxygenated waters for rearing his young by attributing it to instinct. We must look for an immediate cause acting upon the fish himself; and if we take the view that the need for oxygen in the maturing fish grows as his reproductive organs ripen we not only provide ourselves with a perfectly logical and satisfactory explanation of how the fish knows that it must lay its eggs in more vitalized water, but we also give ourselves a clue to the reasons why fish run at certain times and not at others, why certain types of water start all fish in the river moving, and why various atmospheric and natural phenomena have a profound effect upon fish and on fishing.

As an illustration of the vast importance that this question of sufficiency of oxygen is to the young of the genus *Salmo* it may be of interest to consider the process of the hatching of the egg.

The egg is deposited so that it lodges in the crevice between the stones of a redd. The female salmon builds this small edifice with her tail while spawning is in progress for the purpose of providing a home for the eggs where they will at once get a sure and constant supply of fresh water passing over them and at the same time be secure from being washed downstream.

When the egg hatches the young salmon, the alevin, is still in an embryonic state. The egg has hatched in general appearance only. In fact, all that has happened is that the outer casing has ruptured. The embryo fish still has the yolk-sac attached, still relies for nourishment upon the contents of the yolk-sac alone, and is still virtually incapable of individual movement. Why then has the egg hatched? Surely this embryo would be safer inside the egg until he was ready to face the world?

The reason is that, with the growth, the embryo demands an ever-increasing amount of oxygen. The egg has been laid most carefully in a place that will ensure a flow of highly oxygenated water over it, water that will at once provide a maximum of this gas and at the same time carry away CO_2, a product of the respiration in the egg which tends to accumulate in solution round the egg. But there comes a time when, in spite of this provision by the parent fish, the embryo in the shell demands more oxygen than it can get in the restricted quarters that it occupies. Nature has therefore made this not altogether satisfactory compromise and has, for the sake of its easier respiration, allowed the young salmon to hatch out while still an embryo.

The arguments put forward by those who hold that river pollution of a non-poisonous type is not injurious to salmon usually point to the fact that adult fish, and often fry and

31

River Tay—the Ash Pool at Kinnaird. The fisherman is casting a fly over this beautiful stream on the upper Tay while the gillie and a lady watch somewhat critically. And, indeed, they may have noted, first, that the reel is set too high up the handle of the rod; this will imbalance it. Secondly, while his hands are properly placed well apart, his arms are too far away from his body. At this point in a cast the left hand should be almost on the left hip and the right elbow tucked into the waist (*John Tarlton*)

par, are quite demonstrably able to live very comfortably in the polluted water referred to. Pollution that destroys adult fish or even well grown fry is not dangerous, for it is usually so obvious and noxious that it is immediately stopped. The pollution that de-oxygenizes water in the lower and middle reaches beyond the point where young fry can exist in it will cause an immense amount of damage to a salmon river. The pollution that de-oxygenizes the water over the spawning beds, to such an extent that even when prematurely hatched the young embryo fish can no longer breathe, results in the eventual destruction of every salmon in the river. Here is the reason, the specific reason, for the disappearance of salmon from many of our once famous rivers such as the Thames and the Trent.

Water in the pure state is a chemical combination of oxygen and hydrogen. This oxygen, however, is in no sense available to a fish for respiratory purposes. Water, however, is a good solvent of most gases, and pure water dissolves appreciable quantities of all the atmospheric gases. We are only concerned with oxygen at the moment, but may note that nitrogen and, more important, carbon dioxide, are also held in solution in quantity.

The amount of oxygen capable of being held in solution by pure water depends directly upon the temperature and the atmospheric pressure, and a rise of 1°F of temperature drives off between 0.2 and 0.25cc or about $2\frac{1}{2}$ per cent of the total dissolved oxygen.

Many authorities have been led into a number of false conclusions when writing about the oxygen content of water by taking the figures of the saturated solutions as being the normal for all water at the given temperature. This, of course, is untrue. Water does not normally contain dissolved oxygen up to saturation point for a number of reasons, and it is not true to suggest that it is only pollution which reduces the content of oxygen below this point.

The truth of the matter is that the headwaters of the normal river which rises from springs contain practically a saturation point of dissolved gas. As the water flows over the river bed it gets warmed by radiation and conduction in the normal way and accordingly loses the percentage of oxygen proportional to the number of degrees its temperature has been raised. When night comes and the temperature falls this gas is not magically put back into solution. The water tends to re-oxygenate itself by dissolving more gas through the surface, but this is a much slower process than the loss of oxygen, and in consequence, any block of water moving down the river and which starts off by containing a saturated solution of oxygen, loses this gas, for purely mechanical reasons, on the aggregate all the way downstream until it reaches the sea.

So we see that without taking any outside factors into consideration, the natural progress of water down a river is, as far as this factor is concerned, a series of ups and downs with the losses never being made good by the gains.

The speed at which the water will re-oxygenate itself 'mechanically' is dependent upon the amount of surface exposed to the air. In other words, we may say that where a river flows still and deep it will regain much less oxygen overnight or in the cool of the evening than where it flows fast, shallow and broken. Broken water means an enormous increase in surface and a vastly increased rate of re-oxygenation. And here we have a partial reason for the truth of Mr Menzies' statement that temperature and the nature of the river-bed control the running of salmon. They do; not directly but by their effect upon the oxygen content of the water.

Weed and algae, common in the lower reaches of most rivers, give off oxygen during daylight, and absorb CO_2. But in darkness the process is reversed. CO_2 is given off and oxygen is absorbed. A weedy river will become super-saturated with O_2 during the day, and super-saturated with CO_2 and very de-oxygenated at night.

The mechanism by which the oxygen factor affects the fish is through his rate of breathing. The immediate concern of the salmon in the sea is the search for food. Because his physical requirements are unvarying, and the oxygen content of the sea is stable, the fish has no concern for his breathing. In the river, by contrast, the necessity of hunting food has gone, and the main concern of the fish is now respiration. Not only are the demands for oxygen in the ripening fish increasing, but he is living in a medium subject to constant fluctuation in this factor.

The fish breathes, as we have observed, by passing water over his gills. Like any other creature he has a normal muscular rate of breathing; but while a land animal is dependent entirely upon his own muscular energy to inhale air into his lungs, the salmon, in fresh water, is not entirely so. The movement of water in the stream, by causing a flow automatically over his gills, relieves the fish in part of expending energy on breathing. While he is lying in cold and therefore usually well oxygenated water, he needs but little assistance from the stream as his normal rate of breathing is sufficient to pass all the water that is necessary over his gills. When he is lying in warm and less oxygenated water, he moves up into the faster flow in order to save himself from having to breathe more rapidly. And it follows that when he can no longer maintain his normal rate of breathing, even with the help of the flow of the stream, he knows that it is time to move on and he runs.

But while the fish is unwilling to alter the rate of his breathing he is equally unwilling to expend energy on maintaining himself in situ in a very strong current, and he prefers rather to move up the river to a new pool where he can lie in comfort in comparatively slack water than to push up into the very neck of the pool. I believe, as we shall see when we investigate the running fish, that it is instinctive for a fish to conserve his energy as far as possible while he is in the river.

WHY DOES A FISH TAKE?

Let us look for a moment at a fish that has newly arrived in a pool and has settled down in it. He has chosen this pool and this lie in it because he finds there the conditions which his present state of maturity demand. He is absolutely contented. He requires no food, he is breathing easily, and behind a big boulder he is well out of the force of the stream and must do little other than balance himself to maintain his position. Such a fish, I say, cannot be caught by any fair means of fishing!

In common with every fisherman, I have heard, not once, but hundreds of times, some such phrase as 'They won't take till they've settled down', or 'They are off the take because they're unsettled'. Such statements are, I say, the very contradiction of the truth.

Who has not stood on some bridge looking down on perhaps several hundred fish lying in the pool below? They lie in serried ranks quiet, contented, almost motionless; the very picture of disinterestedness and satiety. An angler comes into the pool and starts to cast, and as the fly passes over them do these fish behave in any way as if they were unsettled, do they show the slightest sign of interest, or recognition even of the existence of the fly? Not by the slightest movement do they betray the smallest evidence of any emotion. And if the fly approaches so closely that it is in danger of hitting them, do they turn to attack it? Not at all, they politely move aside and give it a clear passage. They are, in short, not interested. This is the picture of the settled fish under what he regards as normal conditions.

Why then does he sometimes take? My answer is that the settled fish never takes until something happens to unsettle him, and it is to the various factors that may achieve this that the angler must look if he is going to fish in a rational manner.

There are a few well known conditions which are easily recognizable and which are welcomed by the fisherman because they indicate a likelihood of fish taking. A blink of sun and its accompanying warmth on a cold February day, the beginnings of a rise in the water due to rain, the veering of the wind from the east to the west, or the rising of the barometer after a low glass; all these usually mean taking fish. But the logical explanation of why fish take in these circumstances is almost invariably ascribed to some mysterious influence that the reasoning power of man is unable to comprehend.

Yet there is a simple explanation. Each of these atmospheric conditions has a tendency to drive off in one way or another the oxygen in the water and in consequence, to unsettle the fish or a proportion of them. And it is these unsettled fish that have the tendency to take.

During low-water periods of high summer, long daylight causes weed and algae growth to give off free oxygen. The water becomes super-saturated. It is only when darkness comes and the photosynthetic process is reversed that oxygen ceases to be given off and CO_2 takes its place. Now the fish's breathing becomes difficult. He prepares to move; and he can be caught.

RUNNING FISH

I have been brought up, as has every fisherman, on the axiom that 'running fish don't take'. And until fairly recently I accepted this generalization as a true statement of fact. But of late years a different conclusion has been forced upon me. I am now of the opinion that not only can running fish be caught, but that, in fact, the greater proportion of all fish that are caught by the rod are running fish.

May is the great running month in the rivers of the North-East yet, because by now the fish are mostly moving at night, fishermen are apt to forget that at this time nearly all the salmon in the river are on the move. Yet May is without any question the month in which most fish are caught.

Salmon do not run, as many believe, straight from the pool that has held them for a period of time to another where they will stay for several days. We have only to consider the speed at which they run and compare it with the speed at which they swim to realise this.

Anyone who has ever noticed a running fish moving through a pool will agree that the speed at which he swims is considerably faster than a man walking on the bank, a speed which I would estimate to be about 7mph 'bank' speed, or 9mph through the water. In other words, the running fish, if he moves at 7mph would swim 20 miles in about 3 hours' swimming time. But we can observe that, even in a hurry, a running salmon requires about 48 hours to cover this distance, and it follows that the fish is resting for 45 hours out of the 48. The running fish is, then, at rest considerably longer than actually on the move. There is one exception to this. The fish that comes in from the sea in the late summer appears to be in an enormous hurry and undoubtedly travels very fast through the lower stretches. Nevertheless, he too tends to rest most of the day (when like all fish at this time of year he will not take) and run very fast and far at night. But he, too, rests at intervals while actually running. I have caught many fish at Park on the Dee at night in June when fishing for grilse and sea trout—little summer fish that were merely passing through the pool and resting for a few minutes. And it is at these periods of rest that he is, from the fisherman's point of view, at his most vulnerable. This is why May, the great running month, is the best fishing month and why early in the season when fish run only by day, they can only be caught in daylight, while later in the summer, when they run only at night, evening and early morning are the best fishing times.

I think, when we consider how vital it is that a fish should conserve his energy, which is quite irreplaceable while he is in the river, that we should expect him to move in short sharp spurts rather than in a steady slow amble. For we must remember that the river is moving. If it flows at an average speed of 2mph this means that for every hour that the fish swims in it he is covering two miles without the gain of an inch of ground. If the fish is going to swim at a steady $\frac{1}{2}$mph ground speed, or $2\frac{1}{2}$mph water speed whenever he runs, to get to the head-waters of the Dee, for example, 70 miles upstream, he is going to swim for 140 hours. And during this time he will have covered 280 extra miles simply in swimming against the movement of the stream. When we consider a river like the Rhine which is 1,000 miles in length and realize that in this way a salmon would have to swim 5,500 miles to get to the spawning beds, it becomes merely ludicrous. It is obvious that the faster he swims while actually running, the less the effect of the current in increasing his distance, and the less energy he will have to use in getting to his spawning grounds. We have assumed here that the average speed of the current is 2mph. 'Why then', asked a friend to whom I showed this, 'does the fish not expend the same energy when "at rest" in swimming against this current?' The answer is that a fish carefully chooses a place to lie in where he will not have to overcome the flow of the current. There are many misconceptions about the lies of fish. A salmon does not generally lie in swirls or eddies that prevent the water flowing freely past his sides—he requires a smooth flow along the nerves of his median line for his balance. He does, however, lie for preference in an eddy that curls down over his back. Where a big rock sticks out of the water fish rarely lie behind it, but where the river flows over the top, such a rock will provide certain lodges in any pool. It seems that a fish likes to be held down against a stone or the bottom by such a down curving swirl, and the raw red marks, usually under the throat, that are popularly supposed to indicate that a fish has been running hard are in fact caused by the fish being rubbed by such a downward current against a stone on which he has been resting.

While fish tend to run in schools we should be wrong to imagine that when a large number of them leave a pool all together (as they quite often do under certain conditions) they travel in company the whole way. If, for instance, 100 Dee fish all leave the Lawson Pool at Drum, and run roughly to the lower Glentanar water, they do not all rest in the Grey Mare at Blackhall and the Bridge Pool at Potarch and at the same time. Rather the progress of the run is, overall, fairly steady and unchecked. After the first mile or two a proportion of the school starts to drop out and rest in each pool, later to resume running and leap-frogging the others that have gone on ahead. We might say that the run progresses up the river like the tracks of a tank where the links on the ground at any moment represent the resting fish in a succession of pools with the rearmost constantly leap-frogging the others and taking up a new position ahead. And the fish from one pool do not all find their final resting place together in the same new pool higher up the river. A small school, however, which has kept company from the moment of leaving the sea is likely to remain more or less together throughout its river journey. As has been often noted, the big early spring fish and those coming up the river to spawn for the second time tend to run much more slowly and in shorter bursts than the small summer fish, and while the latter spends perhaps several months on or near the spawning bed while still unripe, the former fish do not arrive there until the late autumn.

Experience shows that the length of time during which a fish will take is proportional to how tired he is when he enters the pool and, consequently, on the distance he has run. I have frequently noticed when fishing water in the spring that is as yet unstocked, that the first runs, which are usually fish that have come farther and faster than succeeding runs, will take readily for perhaps as long as three days once they reach the pool that is to be their home, and that subsequent runs that have followed on more slowly will only take in the same pools for a day or less.

The fact that it is salmon that are resting in a pool during the process of running that provides a great proportion of the total bags on any beat during the season, explains the rather curious anomaly that, on an average, more fish are taken in the small streamy pools than in the large, deep, holding pools.

It would appear that running fish have a preference for resting in a type of water in which they are not prepared to lie for any length of time, and that if they do stop in a good holding pool they are likely to settle down and remain there for some time.

A rise in the river level, particularly at periods of low water, by its purely mechanical effect will start a number of fish running. When the river is very low a rise of 3–4in will more than double the volume of water, and even a scarcely measurable rise will have the effect of making many lies untenable. And where a fish already lying in a strong stream cannot find a more sheltered position in his immediate surroundings he will often run even though the rise is brought about by highly oxygenized melted snow water.

3

Practical Applications of the Theory – Fly-Fishing

In the opening chapters we have established a general theory to account for the behaviour of salmon in fresh water, and in particular to indicate the reason for the fish taking at certain times. Having proposed that it is habit that induces a fish to take, that it is an abnormality in his surroundings, particularly a shortage of oxygen, that determines when he will take, and that running fish take readily, it is time to turn to the practical application of this theory. I feel that it is only fair to warn the reader in advance that in logically applying the theoretical conclusions that we have reached to practical fishing, he may be faced with many surprises.

It has already been stated that there is a duality about the life of a salmon in the sea, and that it is upon his habit of hunting and feeding in the ocean that we must rely to catch him in the river. And we have indicated that there is a critical temperature, 48°F, on either side of which the salmon behaves as two entirely different fish. For this reason the fisherman uses two different methods, different tackle, and a different mental approach to his fishing, according to whether the temperature is below or above this point. In the next two chapters we shall forget the warm water summer fishing and confine ourselves to that period when the temperature of the river remains below 48°F. This period of 'spring' fishing extends in the north-east of Scotland to about the middle of April, and it is the season of the sunk line and large fly or baits of anything between 2½in and 4in in length. Why this is so we shall see later in the chapter devoted to salmon flies. Because it is the only item which interests the fish, the fly should be discussed first, but because it is the last item that concerns the angler in his preparation for fishing, we shall discuss the other items of his gear first.

River Blackwater, Ireland. Careysville is arguably the best early spring beat in Ireland, and better in February and March than any beat in Scotland. The Duke of Devonshire owns Careysville and is seen fishing out his cast in this picture. By comparison with our fisherman on the Tay in the previous picture you will note that the reel is correctly placed low down on the handle, that the Duke is relaxed yet concentrating on where his fly is fishing, and that he holds a loop of line ready to let it go if a fish pulls. It should be noted, also, that he is fishing right-handed from the right bank. This, in my view, is the correct shoulder to cast over, but most fishermen believe that casting should probably be over the left shoulder on the right bank (*Sport and General Press Agency*)

GEAR

Rods

In my grandfather's day, rods of 18–20ft were the fashion. They were usually of greenheart, but sometimes of washaba or hickory, and they carried reels and lines proportional to their size. Salmon fishing in those days must have been a rigorous exercise. Largely, if not entirely, due to the invention of the split cane rod, with its great power in proportion to its length, the size of the rods used has decreased greatly of late years, and if my observation is correct, is still decreasing. The 16ft rod is a rarity today, and more and more fishermen are finding that a 14ft rod or even smaller is quite capable of fulfilling their needs.

The choice of a rod for spring fishing is, unlike that for greased-line fishing, governed not so much by considerations of comfort and fancy as by the very strenuous demands that will be made upon it in casting a 3in fly and in lifting a heavy line from deep in the water. But those who believe that a shorter rod requires less effort in casting than a larger rod are much mistaken. A 15ft rod is much less tiring to fish with than a 13ft. And ladies should never be asked to fish with shorter rods than men.

Handles

It is well worthwhile, too, having a handle made that is most to your liking. As with most sporting implements there is a great variety of tastes in this, but the rod-maker, for the most part, disregards this fact and fits a standard handle on all his goods. I find, for instance, that the cork handle as fitted in the shop is too big for my liking and I have it filed down to suit my grip. Others like a bigger handle than the average. Some like a handle that is thickest at the grip and fines down as it merges into the rod. I prefer it to be rather thicker above the grip. These are all small points that can be easily adjusted to suit the individual; but they are so often forgotten or disregarded. I have found too, that a big sorbo rubber button, almost the size of a tennis ball, fitted in place of the normal hard rubber button is a great comfort when playing fish.

Reels

The most important point in a reel is that it should have a variable check on the ratchet. When fishing with a heavy cast and in strong water, it is annoying to find that unless the drum is checked by the fingers, the line is taken out by the force of the stream alone. It is, too, quite impossible to maintain satisfactory contact with a hooked fish. Under these circumstances, a fairly strong check on the running of the reel is essential. On the other hand, a heavy ratchet, should you be using a fine cast, can be fatal. Most reels are made nowadays with a spare ratchet incorporated in the works. It is well worth paying a little extra for this, since having to fish with a reel in which the ratchet is broken is a tedious performance and most trying to the temper.

Lines

Lines come in all shapes and sizes. And upon the choice of his line will depend not only much of the angler's comfort, but to a large extent the number of fish that he catches. The first essential for spring fishing is that the line shall be heavy. Nowadays there is not much to choose in this respect between the lines of one maker and another, though I think that the oil-dressed lines are perhaps slightly heavier. But whether they be green, brown, yellow, or even white, is probably a matter of individual preference. The rod-maker will supply, if given a chance, a line which he states is properly balanced for the rod. From experience I have found that this is invariably a line that is a size, or in extreme cases, two sizes too light. The maker is more concerned to ensure the life of his rods than the comfort of the fisherman. A heavy line is essential for spring fishing, firstly, because it must sink, and secondly, because casting a light line, that is, a line which will not make the rod work down to the butt, is exhausting at any time and impossible in a wind.

Allowing that every fisherman now uses a tapered line, there are two types of line from which a choice may be made. The most common is the standard double tapered with the first 18–20yd gently tapered off from the maximum, usually about 6yd in the centre. The line tapers off in exactly the same manner to its rear and can be reversed on the reel without affecting its properties. The other type is a line that has a very sudden taper at one end with its maximum diameter about 20ft from the cast and tapering off rapidly again to a considerable length of line little heavier than a spinning line. This line can be fished only at one end and cannot be reversed on the reel, but it is very easy to cast and to shoot.

The virtue of the cast is not so much in preventing the fish noticing the line, for I believe that the salmon, even if he sees it, does not associate the line with danger in any shape or form, but in allowing the fly to sink deep and in giving it a very free play in the water. For this reason, too, the greatest success will always be achieved with the finest cast that can safely be fished. With the large fly it is not the strength of the water nor yet the size of the fish that will determine this, but the fact that a 3in fly cannot be cast with very fine gut without eventually breaking it. While no two fishermen will have the same ideas on this question of the thickness of gut at any particular time, and while I do not believe that fish are, except in very rare cases, gut shy, there is one definite limitation on the thickness of cast used. Having regard to the strength of the water which is being fished, the cast must never be so thick that it will prevent the fly swinging perfectly naturally in the eddies of the current. A fly that does not swing freely into the eddies loses much of its quality of flashing (see page 11).

Waders

Unless you are going to fish exclusively out of a boat or on a beat where there is only bank fishing you will need waders. And, remembering that you will be spending perhaps more than eight hours a day in them six days a week, it is well worth paying a small amount extra to have them made for you. I have found that most waders are made too short in the leg for comfort and that a pair that is actually too long in this respect is far more comfortable to walk in than even waders of the correct length. It is a distinct economy to have two pairs in use at the same time, since wearing them in turn gives the pair not being worn ample time to dry out properly.

Because all waders, even in deep water, do contain a certain amount of air in them in spite of the pressure of the water, the type that fastens round the waist, either with a running cord or a belt, can be dangerous. The fisherman who falls in even in shallow water wearing waders so fastened, can very easily be drowned because water cannot get into the waders to displace the air, and in consequence his legs are liable to float, and his head go down.

Thick understockings, preferably two pairs of them, materially assist in keeping the feet warm.

Extras

Apart from flies, which require a chapter to themselves, the fly-fisherman with a rod, reel, line, cast, waders, stockings and boots, has now all that is absolutely necessary to set forth and catch fish. But without any doubt, like myself, he will spend many happy hours thumbing through those delightfully illustrated tackle-maker's catalogues and writing off for a dozen-and-one extras, most of which, attractive as they seem on paper, will be found superfluous on the riverside.

Of these I would recommend a pair of scissors, polarized glasses, a small fine carborundum stone for sharpening hooks,

River Blackwater, Careysville. Here we have a lady, the Duchess of Devonshire, playing and landing a fish on a spinning rod. She has a drum reel carrying a plaited silk thread line and she is using it on top of the rod, not underneath. A most experienced fisherman, the Duchess is probably being annoyed by the advice which her gillie is, clearly, freely tendering, but the onlooker is wisely keeping out of the way. Note that the fish is gaffed over the back and not from underneath, but the gillie is going to knock it on the head with his priest while still on the gaff. This may tear the fish, even cause it to be dropped, so the Duchess is wisely winding in the line and keeping contact with her fish. The dog—oddly for a labrador—has lost all interest (*Sport and General Press Agency*)

and a line drier, as the most useful. At the period of the change-over from sunk- to greased-line fishing, a thermometer is quite essential, but if carried about in a fishing bag must be of the enclosed metal type, otherwise it is certain to get broken. A gaff, I find, is an encumbrance, and in any case, as we shall see later, the times when it should be used are so few and far between that it is not worth carrying. A wading stick gives confidence to the elderly.

WHERE TO FISH

The next consideration is where to fish. Most of us are not the owners of a beat on a salmon river and we must take one, therefore, for the period of our holiday. This is a process full of pitfalls for the unwary.

Fishing agents I find singularly uninformed, as a class, about the wares they are offering and their knowledge of the beat that they hope you will take usually begins and ends with what is printed on a sheet of foolscap paper. This is generally little more than a summary of the bags over a dozen seasons, the names of the pools and the rent asked—and it is not enough.

If you are planning to take a fortnight, say in March, you should insist on knowing the average catches during this month over a period of years. It may sound elementary to point it out but there are many excellent beats with large annual bags in which the first fish are seldom taken before April. And if you prefer the substance to the shadow you will take a beat that shows steady takes every year. If you prefer a gamble, you will take a beat where the average bag is made up by a few outstanding seasons amongst several bad ones. In this case, unless you have some reliable inside information, you will have to face the possibility of finding yourself on a beat with no fishable pools with the water above a certain height in a month when the river never runs out of spate. This has happened to me and so I speak with some feeling.

50

It is a false economy as a general rule to take cheap fishing. At the present moment, when rents have rocketed, the letting value of a beat is assessed at £30–40 per fish. If you have a fortnight in the year and are taking a single rod for yourself, you will have to pay perhaps more than £200 a week for the best fishing. For indifferent or bad fishing you will have to pay perhaps £40 a week. In the first instance only the most execrable ill-fortune will prevent you catching a dozen fish in your fortnight and you have always a chance of striking lucky and killing perhaps thirty or forty. In the latter instance the best you can hope for is a half-dozen. You will have several blank days and will have no reason to feel aggrieved if your total bag amounts to but one or two fish.

When you consider, too, that the overheads, that is hotel expenses, journeys, gillies' wages, and cost of tackle, remain the same in both good and bad fishing, it becomes quite apparent that, the question of the enjoyment you will get aside, it is cheapest in the long run to take the very best fishing that is procurable.

It is, incidentally, worthwhile working out just what your chances of catching fish really are when considering a fortnight's holiday on an expensive beat. As a young man when taking a rod on, say, the Aberdeenshire Dee, I knew that, if it were a four-rod beat on the middle part of the river whose annual bags averaged 500 fish, these fish would all be taken in the four months from February to the end of May, and that about half of them would be caught between 15 April and 15 May. In a May fortnight my chances would be roughly twenty-five fish. In March about twelve fish would be my share. And on average it worked out about right.

Today, however, if offered a similar beat with a 400 fish bag, I would have to reckon that these fish were taken over a period of about nine months, a high proportion indeed being caught in September. My chances in the same May fortnight would certainly be halved and probably reduced to a quarter.

In the Spey, too, some of the most highly rented beats which we used to fish with four rods and only in the spring and early summer, now have over twenty rods on the same water and fishing solidly throughout the nine months of the season. Your real chance here is often less than one fish per week—very expensive fishing.

Another fact to remember is that from the point of view of your pleasure, it is infinitely better to take a short beat with both banks than a longer beat with more pools, but which you can only fish from one side. Nothing can be more maddening than to discover that the tenant on the other side uses nothing but, say, the prawn. Many of the Scottish rivers, virtually all the Dee and much of the Tay, for instance, have beats with single bank fishing. In Ireland a more rational view is taken. Most beats on the great Irish rivers have both banks—a 'must' for maximum enjoyment of the sport.

4

Fishing the Sunk Fly – Strategy

Equipped with rod and line, with well-fitting waders and with a box of flies together with some nylon for casts, it is time to go fishing on the very expensive beat we have just taken.

The gillie is hopeful. He has seen clean fish showing in the pool, the day is warm and not too bright, and the water at a good spring height and about 40°F.

CHOICE OF FLY

The first problem which poses itself is the choice of fly. The problem that confronts the angler when choosing a fly is the basic problem in salmon fishing. It is curious to reflect that, whereas the fisherman has spent possibly more than £200 on his tackle, rent, and overhead expenses for a week's holiday, it is only a few shillings' worth of feathers and a hook that is of any interest to the fish. We have established that it is habit and not fear, curiosity, anger or that the fly represents a creature in distress, that makes a salmon take. And from circumstantial evidence we have built up a rough picture of the specific creature on which the salmon is accustomed to feeding at this time of year in the ocean. We have said that it is somewhere between 3 and 4in long, tenuous, and possibly with some flashing mark upon it. The successful fly must, therefore, in the vastly different conditions of the river, convey

53

to the salmon the appearance of a creature of this sort.

The first necessity, therefore, in the fly is that it shall conform with this hypothetical prey of the salmon in size. And the use of small flies in early spring, more particularly those of under 2in, is both illogical and unfruitful.

The evolution of the salmon fly is fairly obvious. Salmon were big fish and they rose like trout. Trout took flies of a definite shape and character. Salmon also would take flies of the same sort but, being bigger fish, a bigger fly was needed —and it was successful. The salmon fly started life as a big trout wet fly. And it has remained true to this general characteristic to this day.

The sizes between 1½in and 2½in will occasionally kill fish, but it is only the very keen salmon that will bother to take them. The bulk of the taking fish disregard them, both because they are not a reasonable representation of the creature they are used to hunting in this temperature of water and because they are too small to sink within easy reach. I will guarantee firstly, that any fisherman who will use nothing but 3in or bigger flies throughout the spring and until the river temperature rises to 48°F will catch half as many fish again in any Scottish river as he would catch by changing down to smaller sizes as the water warmed or fell.

Not only because it conforms in size with the salmon's winter prey in the sea is the 3in fly the minimum size with the sunk line, but also because smaller flies than this, even in low water, will not sink deeply enough even with a heavy line.

WHAT THE FISH SEES

The spring salmon is prepared to take a lure that behaves somewhat in the manner of a small fish swimming in deep water. The summer salmon looks for his prey nearly on the surface. And it is due largely to the peculiar effects of the refraction of light in water and to the reflecting properties of the surface that it is absolutely essential that the sunk fly must be kept well away from the surface of the water.

Allowing for the moment that the salmon has an eye which sees much the same as a man, we will examine a fish lying 7ft below the surface in a quiet pool. If you will accept my word for it that the refractive index of water is 1.5 to 1 and that therefore any light which enters the water from nearly parallel to the surface is bent downwards through an angle of 48½°, you will see that the salmon cannot see through the surface at any angle greater than 41½° from the vertical. In other words, the fish sees the brightness of the sky through a round hole with an arc of 83° in the surface of the water, or in the case of the fish we are discussing, through a hole whose diameter is about 13ft. Beyond this angle the surface of the water acts as a mirror and reflects only the bed of the river or anything moving in the water below the surface.

Now a fish that is feeding in deep water in the sea is not aware of any surface, for it is too far away to affect him in any way. The prey that such a fish hunts is seen directly through the water. A fish feeding near the surface, on the other hand, is very well aware of the peculiarity of the behaviour of light and of the reflecting property of the surface which, for practical purposes, is partial as he looks at it at any angle beyond 30° from the vertical, and becomes total at 41½°. Indeed, the easiest way in which a fish can see an object that is near the surface but beyond an angle of 41½° from the vertical is to look at the surface and see its reflection.

In the case of our fish lying 7ft below the surface of the water, let us look at a fly 9ft away from him in the horizontal plane and 1ft below the surface. This fly, seen directly, is rather over 11ft from the fish who is looking upwards at the underparts of the fly which are illuminated only by the reflected light from the bottom of the river and any scattered light due to impurities in the water. This fly is seen against a reflection of the bottom of the river which, because it is illuminated by direct overhead light, is brighter in tone than the underparts of the fly. Even though looking in this direction and being aware of this rather insignificant ill-lit object, the attention of the fish is distracted by something far more exciting. At a slight inclination to the vertical from it, and apparently 2ft further distant, is another fly. This one is brightly lit and full of colour and flash. To it is imparted a certain nebulous appearance, as if seen through a glass of uneven thickness. It is in very truth a dream fly. But, alas, it is an illusion. This exciting object is the reflection of the real fly seen against the uneven mirror of the surface of the water. It is brightly illuminated because now it is the top of the fly that is reflected. And when we remember that the fish has always a bright light shining down into those lidless eyes from an arc of over 80° directly above him, it is little wonder that a dimly illustrated object like your fly when seen directly through the water is probably not noticed if there is a far more attractive morsel so close to it.

When fishing with the sunk fly it is of paramount importance that the reflection of the fly should never be so near to the true image that they can be associated with each other. When fishing the greased line it is essential that the reflection and the fly itself be seen together and as, virtually, one object. In this sentence, I say, the whole art of salmon fly-fishing is crystallized.

When fishing with the sunk fly, why is it so important that the reflection of the fly should be kept away from the reality? First, because, as we have said, in his natural feeding ground, the sea, the salmon is hunting during the winter in water where there is, virtually, no surface. I do not necessarily mean to assert that he is feeding in very deep water, but only in water of such a depth that the surface is too far away to matter. He is, as we have said, feeding on a small fish of 3–4in in length. This he sees, of necessity, directly and not very brightly illuminated. We may surmise that he sees this creature on his own level as a rule and not from below. He does not see

River Shin, Sutherland—The Falls Pool. The fisherman in our picture
has problems! First, overhead casting is impossible so he has to spey
cast, left handed. Secondly, when he has hooked his fish he has to land
him and he cannot move from where he is standing. He has also to
be careful not to fall in himself. To hook a big fish in such a pool,
to play him and land him is the dream of every angler (*L. S. Paterson*)

57

any reflection of this creature.

When we attempt to catch the salmon in the river we set out to do so by playing on the assumption that under certain circumstances we can induce the fish to revert to the habit of his sea life. We attempt to stimulate his memory and an instinctive reversion to habit. We must, therefore, present our fly so that it appears to the fish in the very different surroundings of the river as much like his winter sea prey as possible. And the moment we allow a brightly illuminated reflection to be associated with the reality of the fly we are destroying all the illusion of any memory of feeding in a 'surfaceless' ocean.

It is a strange anomaly that most fishermen are quite content to put on the biggest fly in their box when the water is heavy or dirty; but when the river falls and clears they will use progressively smaller and smaller sizes of fly. In heavy, dirty water the surface ceases to be important to a fish as the light entering the water gets diffracted by the impurities to such an extent that the mirror-like properties are dissipated. There is, consequently, comparatively little danger of the reflection of the fly being seen. The lower and clearer the water, the more vivid the reflection compared with the reality and the farther he will see both the fly and the image in reflection. In low, clear water it is more important than ever to fish a big fly and to fish as deeply as possible. In a strong stream it is, of course, impossible to sink the fly as deeply as one would like. Nature, however, provides as usual a safety device. The surface of such streams is almost invariably rippled or otherwise disturbed, and is consequently unable to act like a mirror. It is notoriously difficult to catch spring fish in those strong, glassy glides at the tails of certain pools, but comparatively easy to do so in the summer with the greased line.

In the normal way I have observed that spring fish are very loath to rise to a fly. And I think that this is due to the fact that, when hunting in deep water in the ocean, the salmon views his prey at nearly his own level, turns so that he gets a stereoscopic view of it with both eyes and, having now determined its distance from him, seizes it. He does not get under it and rise to it for there is no point in so doing. Nor is it necessary for him to see his prey outlined against a strong light.

For these reasons the best success with the sunk fly comes when it is presented in such a manner that it passes in front of the fish near enough for him to see it clearly, low enough in the water to ensure that its reflection, if seen, is not associated with it, and also low enough for it to pass into the arc of stereoscopic vision in front of the fish but not into the cone of bright light that lies above him. It would seem, too, that the reflexes of the fish in very cold water are much slower than in warm, and that the stimulus required to make a fish take is considerably greater. While in the summer the sight of a fly at a considerable distance will rouse him, in the spring the lure must approach far more closely to have the same effect. A large fly, a heavy line and a deep and slow style of fishing are, I repeat, the key to successful cool-water fishing.

COLOURS AND TONES

The question of the value of various colours and patterns of salmon flies is one that is constantly recurrent and one on which widely divergent views are held. I think that most fishermen have felt that to suppose that the salmon should differentiate between, say, a Black Doctor and a Thunder and Lightning was faintly ridiculous; and the more modern school of thought is tending all the time, largely as a result of the experiences of greased-line fishing, to the belief that colour is of little importance in the salmon fly.

From the study of the construction of a fish's eye we would expect that he would be rather insensitive to colour, rather incapable of deciding exact shapes and size but exceptionally sensitive to movement. And we should expect that as darkness

59

fell his vision would remain acute and nearly his normal for a long time.

We are, of course, taking a good deal for granted in suggesting that the fish sees in the same manner as we do. For instance, it is perfectly conceivable that the fish may be entirely receptive to colour as far as his eye is concerned, but quite incapable of discriminating or judging between colours in his brain. After all, what the human eye sees, and what the human brain takes in, are two entirely different matters. We may also suggest with fair certainty that:

1 He is aware of the general shape of an object anywhere within his arc of vision equally well, but that no object is ever in distinct focus and that its outlines are never defined clearly.

2 Until he can view an object stereoscopically with both eyes he has no means of computing more than very roughly its distance from himself or its size.

3 He will notice the movement of any object within the arc of his vision extremely quickly.

4 His vision in bad light is comparatively acute and in a strong light likely to be bad owing to his inability to use the iris of his eye as a shutter.

Generalizing then, we may say that the salmon is myopic and colour-blind, but that he is sensitive to tone and very sensitive to movement. And in our choice of fly we must attempt to represent to a fish with the above peculiarities of vision an accurate copy in the different surroundings of the river of a creature that he has only seen in the gloom of the deep sea.

Colour, then, can have little effect, for it is the tone of the fly that is important. And for this reason the colour of the wing of the sunk salmon fly is of little importance save in giving a certain tenuous bulk to the thin body. The hackle, because it is usually composed of dyed feathers, has rather more effect on the tone, but also contributes towards the tenuousness of the fly in the water. But the greater factor influencing the general tone of the fly is without any doubt

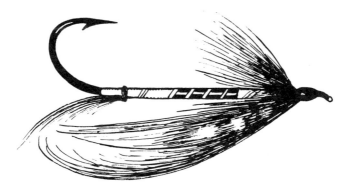

Fig 1

the body. And it is in the body, too, that we shall simulate that little flash of brightness that is the most noticeable feature of any moving fish (Fig 1).

I have stressed this question of tone as against that of colour because, as experience has shown, fish will take flies of almost any colour, but the old saying 'a bright fly for a bright day' proves to be correct more often than not. The reason for this is that when we speak of tone, we do not mean the actual tone of the fly, but the comparative tone. We are, in fact, somewhat in the position of the artist painting a picture who wants to put in a shadow of the right values. He paints his shadow heavily or lightly not so much with regard to the number of foot candles of light in the particular shadow in reality, but having regard to the sensation of shadow it will give the beholder when compared unconsciously with the tone of the surroundings. So we choose a fly, not that is of the same tone as the salmon's natural prey, but one which, under the conditions of light prevalent at the time, will give the illusion to the salmon of being of the same tone.

Here, however, there is a somewhat odd inversion. The fish, whose memory of fat feeding days you are attempting to stimulate, has lived and eaten in surroundings which have little variation in light and shade from one day to the next. The background colour of an object in the sub-surface layers of the sea is almost unchanging. Consequently we must try to reproduce in our fly the same tonal value compared with its changing surroundings as a small fish would have in the unchanging surroundings of the deeper sea. In other words, whereas you or I would expect a grey sheep to appear black when seen against snow, or grey when seen in a green field of the same tonal value as itself, and nearly white seen against the dark background of heather, and we would say that it was unsheep-like if it appeared otherwise, the salmon, on the other hand, has always, when feeding, seen his food as, say, grey because the background has never changed. If, therefore, you now change the background tone, you must also change the tone of the fly so that it always appears grey.

This I consider the fundamental requirement of any salmon fly and also of spinning baits. It should always have a constant tonal value when seen against its background. If the background is bright and well lit, then the fly or bait must be bright or it will appear too dark. When the background is dark and ill lit, then the lure must be dark or it will appear to be too bright.

Unfortunately we do not know the exact tone of the salmon's real prey any more than we know what its exact shape or colour is. We have, however, very strong circumstantial evidence born of centuries of experience that tells us that, in regarding the fly as a normal type of small fish, ie with a bright belly and dark back, we are not far off the track, and our only problem is to maintain its relative tone against that of its background. The answer can be condensed into the time-worn truism 'The brighter the day the brighter the fly'.

In theory, if one accepts the hypothesis that salmon behave as if not colour conscious, a self-coloured fly of the correct tone should be every bit as successful as flies of variegated colours. In practice this is almost certainly not the case. And the reason, in my opinion, is that unless the standard fly is camouflaged its outline becomes too exact and it ceases to look like the rather shadowy illusion of its own prey that the salmon takes it to be. The value of different colours in a fly is that they tend to break up the outline and solidity of the fly and to create an illusion of life and movement. The topping of golden pheasant which lies along the upper edge of the wing of so many flies is an excellent example of the camouflaging of an outline. It is thin, shimmering and evanescent. At a casual glance you cannot tell where the outline of the wing begins and ends. The fly is a living creature because of this. And it is the same throughout the wing, the body and the hackles of salmon flies. The different colours break up the outlines, transform a monstrosity of steel and feathers into a creature of life and movement.

REPRESENTING A FISH

We have already indicated that the trout wet fly does not usually represent a fly, but rather either a nymph or a fish. The salmon fly definitely does not represent an insect—it is too big—but almost certainly represents a fish. Let us look at it for a moment.

At first glance there does not appear to be anything very fish-like about this object. Let us, however, remove the hook (Fig 2). This still does not look much like a fish. So let us try again. Let us put this object of feathers into the water and hold it steady against a current flowing past it. By sketching in the missing portions we now have an object which gives a very fair representation of a fish (Fig 3). And when we remember that all salmon flies without exception have bright or partly bright bodies which represent the light underparts of a fish, we can see how our fly, with the hook acting as a keel and keeping it right way up, can deceive the salmon fairly successfully.

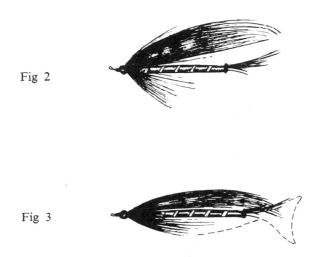

Fig 2

Fig 3

He is a creature who demands little from his environment —neither food nor drink, shelter nor warmth. He has, comparatively, but a short journey in front of him, and several months in which to accomplish it. His one desire, it seems, is to be left in peace. Nevertheless you, my friend, have the presumption to throw such an outrageous object as a salmon fly into the water and expect our replete and entirely self-contained fish to remove himself from a comfortable lodge and, at the cost of no little effort, seize and make off with an object of which he can neither have previous cognizance nor any possible need. Now is this a logical or even intelligent approach to the sport of salmon fishing? Surely it is not; nevertheless it is the normal approach of many salmon fishermen in this country today.

SPEED

If your fly represents a fish of about $2\frac{1}{2}$–3in in length it must, fairly obviously if the illusion is to be preserved, move through the water somewhat after the manner of a small fish in similar conditions.

If you observe any small fish either in an aquarium or in a pond or lake swimming about in the normal course of its daily life, you will see that it does, in fact, swim very slowly, about 2–3 mph.

Of course there will be individual differences in speed between different species of small fish, but these are not likely to be of more than a magnitude of 50 per cent one way or the other, and if we place the maximum sustained swimming speed of the hypothetical prey of the salmon at $4\frac{1}{2}$mph and its normal speed at less than 3mph we shall probably not be too far out.

Your fly then, if it is going to resemble a small fish, should move through the water at never more than $4\frac{1}{2}$mph and, preferably, at less than 3mph.

But consider just what this means. Your fly cast out at an angle into the river has two speeds. The one is relative to yourself or to the bank or the bottom of the river, the other is relative to the water. Standing on land you are apt to regard the speed of your fly as the speed with which it swings round from midstream against the force of the current and at the

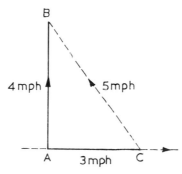

Fig 4 'True speed' of fly

same time edging in sideways towards the bank. The speed at which the fly is moving is, to the fish, a combination of its lateral and horizontal speeds. It is the resolved factor of both.

If we draw a simple diagram (Fig 4) where AB represents the speed of flow of the water (4mph) and AC represents the speed at which the fly swings sideways towards the bank (3mph), we can see that the true speed of the fly is represented by BC; and by our old friend Pythagoras is in fact $(4^2 + 3^2)$, or 5mph, and the fly is therefore not fishing properly. It is moving faster than any little fish of such a size could move.

This question of the true speed of the fly is possibly the most fundamental factor in successful fishing, and it is equally as true of the sunk-line as of the greased-line methods. Not nearly enough attention is paid to it.

I should say that, generally speaking, with the sunk-line the most success will be achieved when the fly moves at rather under than over 3mph in true speed and that it should be the first concern of the fisherman to preserve the illusion he is creating by keeping the fly's speed down as far as possible to this figure.

By the same token, of course, in absolutely slack water the true speed drops away and if not maintained by artificial methods, such as hand-lining or lifting the rod point, the illusion again is destroyed. Here, of course, the bait scores because it is being moved, while winding-in is in progress, at approximately the right speed.

DIRECTION

At the same time as considering speed, we must also consider the direction in which the fly moves. This, at first, may appear a silly suggestion. The fly, you may say, obviously moves in the direction in which it is going. But in fact, unless some care is taken, for the greater part of the fishing time of any cast, the fly does not move in the direction in which it is apparently going.

If a fly is moving from X to Y (Fig 5) at a bank speed of 3mph across a current of 4mph we have seen that its true water speed is 5mph. Likewise, a fish swimming (or a man swimming or rowing a boat for that matter) direct from X to Y at 3mph, cannot turn its head directly to Y as it will get carried downstream. It must, in fact, point itself along the axis XO in our Fig 5 and keep swimming forward at this angle to the current. This is a very elementary principle in navigation, and a fish if it wanted to move along the line XY would have to conform to this principle. Your fly must, therefore, also conform and must point the right way.

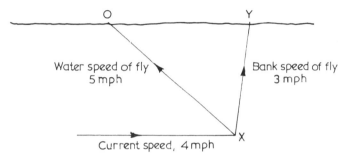

Fig 5 'Pointing' the fly correctly

But we are immediately confronted with a complication which renders the achievement of this desired object difficult of attainment. If our fly were held at the end of a long inflexible rod such as a pendulum, it would swing round in the stream always pointing roughly in the desired direction. But, in fact, we attach it to the end of a long, thin line which, when cast across a stream, immediately becomes curved in a 'belly'. The result of this on the fly is twofold. First, while the belly is still forming, the speed of the fly remains normal, then when the belly becomes pronounced, the fly undergoes acceleration, and finally it may achieve such a speed that it is dragged through the water at a constant speed far in excess of what it ought to be.

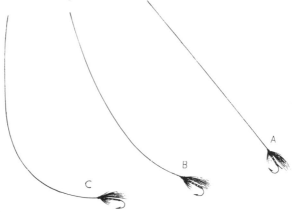

Fig 6

Far worse, if indeed anything could be worse, are the changes in the direction of the axis of the fly (Fig 6). At A, the fly is newly cast and the line and fly are now all pointing in the proper and natural direction. As the belly forms (position B) the fly, though still moving at about the same speed, is pulled off its proper axis and begins to crab-walk sideways through the water. When this belly becomes very pronounced as in C, the fly now moves square across the current in a manner absolutely impossible of achievement by anything not, in fact, attached to a line and being dragged.

The point of all this is that whereas you may cast perfectly and fish your fly apparently perfectly over every foot of water, you may, in fact, be showing the fish a reasonable representation of his prey which, because it moves in a manner in which no living creature could move, has lost all similarity to the little fish the salmon is looking for. A 'belly' on the line can be the deadly enemy to successful fishing. It can also, as we shall see, become a useful artifice in the armoury of the fisherman who understands when and where to use it.

From these observations emerges the first and most important general rule for successful fly-fishing. It is that the fly must be fished slowly, so slowly that in currents of above 4mph it should scarcely move, and that it must be kept pointing along an axis which conforms to the direction in which a fish should have to swim if wishing to cross the stream at the same pace as does the fly.

HORIZONTAL AXIS

The next point that requires consideration is that of the horizontal axis of the fly. Fish swim level; that is to say, their main axis lies in an exact horizontal plane and not at an angle to it. Does your fly also conform to this?

The problem confronting the angler is how to fish his fly slowly and at the same time keep it level in the water. It

River Garry, Invernesshire—the mouth of the river. The Garry fish which average seventeen pounds are early running and travel straight through the Ness, Loch Ness, the river Oich into Loch Oich where they wait to run the Garry. This is a distance of some forty miles and fresh fish are always in Loch Oich and this pool on the opening day, 15 January (*William B. Currie*)

becomes fairly obvious that in fast-flowing water the frictional force of the stream is sufficient normally to maintain this fly in its correct position. But in slack water, unless movement is imparted to the fly, it will tend to drop away from the horizontal to an extent proportional to the speed of the current.

Furthermore, it is equally obvious that the normal single-hooked salmon fly which has its wing set at an angle to the body (or shank of the hook) can only be a compromise, in the sense that it will only swim on an apparently horizontal keel in one speed of current. If the water flows faster than this, then the fly will give the appearance of a small fish swimming downhill; if the current be slower, then the illusion will be of a fish swimming to the surface.

It must be pointed out also in the same connection that the line and cast play no small part in maintaining the fly on its correct axis, or otherwise. A light line and a cast which tends to float obviously tends to lift the head of the fly; and it is partly for this reason that big spring flies cannot be fished successfully on light lines.

WEIGHT

The question of weight in spring salmon flies is also one of major importance. Spring flies must be heavy and they must be fished deep. Consider where the fish is lying and why it is lying there.

The early spring fish chooses for preference the deeper pools and apparently the slacker parts of such pools to lie in. Depth, I am quite certain, has a vast attraction for fish, but I am not sure that the tendency to lie in slack water is not more an illusion observed by the angler than a reality. It must be remembered that, at any rate in most Scottish salmon rivers, the normal winter and spring levels are between 1ft and 1ft 6in above the summer levels and that in such rivers as the Dee or Spey this implies a volume of water between three and four times as great as in summer. This, in turn, means an average speed of flow of rather more than double that of the same river in summer. The effect upon the observer is something in the nature of an optical illusion. When looking at a pool in low water he sees the stream running at, say, 6mph at its head, dropping away gradually to perhaps less than 1mph at the sides and slack water in the middle of the pool. He now notes that the fish are lying just off or behind the main stream. Seeing the same pool at winter level he observes the stream now running at 12mph or more, and dropping away as before to less than 1mph. The fish may still be lying in that part of the river where the water flows at 3–5mph—but this, in comparison with the main stream, appears to be very slack water, an illusion that is enhanced by the fact that it is also probably much nearer to the bank.

In point of fact, I believe that spring fish will and do lie in very much heavier currents than is generally supposed. The key to this apparent anomaly lies in the choice of lodges exercised by the individual fish. Because the surface and intermediate layers of the stream are flowing fast there is no justification for suggesting that the bottom layer of water is necessarily moving at even half this speed.

Friction and turbulence, due to the uneven bottom of a typical salmon pool, will create even in the strongest streams, areas of calm, of slight current and even of reverse currents; for the moment it will suffice to say that one of the problems of presentation of the fly to a fish lying in hard water is that of inducing him to leave the shelter of the comparative slack in which he is lying on the bottom, and to face the full strength of the current to get the fly. This turns out to be a virtual impossibility save in exceptional circumstances. The alternative, therefore, is to get the fly down to the fish. Here, then, is the reason why at all times spring flies must be heavy. It is useless to use flies of the right size and appearance if, because they are too light, they never fish in a place to which the salmon is prepared to sally forth to take them.

71

5

Greased-Line Fishing

Fly-fishing in late spring and summer is a very different matter from what is euphemistically described as 'spring fishing' but which is effectively winter fishing in cold weather, poor light and in heavy cold water.

The change, usually towards the end of April, is signalled by the rise in temperature of the river water to a degree or two above a critical point of 48°F. When the water achieves this the salmon, who also acquires the same temperature, appears to undergo a change of habit and outlook. He is no longer interested in sizeable flies and baits fished well away from the surface. He now looks at the surface of the pool and his curiosity and, perhaps, appetite, is whetted by something far smaller which moves in the upper layers of the water. Just as the salmon behaves as an entirely different fish when his surroundings are more than 48°F, so must the fisherman approach him with a new outlook, new methods and changed equipment.

For the fly-fisherman the basic difference lies in the size of the fly used. The fact that flies of less than 1in in length are used in place of those of $2\frac{3}{4}$–3in affects every item of equipment. The small fly requires a fine cast to carry it, a line light enough to float, and a rod and reel suitable for fishing with light tackle.

It is convenient to leave the matter of flies and fly sizes until later and to begin our examination of the tackle requirements with the line.

THE GREASED LINE

This line is essentially a compromise. It must be light or it will not, even when amply greased, float. But it must also be heavy enough to be cast in comfort even in a wind. The heaviest line which, in my experience, will float is No 5 Kingfisher or its equivalent. A No 4 floats better, but I prefer the trouble of frequent drying and greasing a somewhat heavy line to the discomfort occasioned by the unmanageability of a lighter line which requires little greasing.

The rod must be designed to suit the line. Again we face the same problems that confront us in the choice of rods for spring fishing. Either we may have a short, powerful rod which can only be used by a powerfully-built man, or we can have a longer and less powerful rod suitable for the average fisherman, or a still longer and weaker rod suitable for a lady or the man of less than average physique.

It remains, therefore, merely to detail the exact sizes. The shortest practicable size of rod for use with a No 5 Kingfisher is a 12ft rod. A 12ft 6in rod would suit most men better, and a rod of between 13ft and 13ft 6in is more comfortable and would certainly be correct for a lady.

There is an unfortunate impression, created I think by a precedent set by the late Arthur Wood at Cairnton, that a 12ft rod can be used single-handed. I say, unequivocally, that it cannot. Naturally an odd cast can be made single-handed with it just as an odd cast can be made single-handed with a 13ft 6in rod. Naturally, too, if the 12ft rod is made thin and whippy and fitted with a trout line it can be used single-handed. Few of the old-fashioned trout rods of my grand-father's day were less than 11ft 6in and they were used single-handed. But I have yet to meet the man who can wade the

73

Spey or the Dee for a whole day and cast a reasonably long line of No 5 size with a 12ft rod single-handed. Mr Wood fished single-handed with a 12ft rod, it is true. But first, he never had to cast a long line for more than the odd throw at Cairnton; second, he used a line which was far too light for ordinary use, and third, although a strong man, whenever I saw him he used to take long rests at frequent intervals.

But for the fact that distance, or rather the ability to achieve it, is every bit as desirable in greased-line as in sunk-line fishing, it would be tempting to suggest that a trout rod

River Lochy and Ben Nevis. This is one of the true late summer and autumn rivers of the west coast which is not a spate river. Fed by the lochs of the Lochiel country and the streams of the Ben Nevis mountains, the Lochy is never too low for fish to run. The Mucomer Pool, below the junction with the Spean, is unfailingly good in August and September and the whole river yields fresh fish at a time of year when few fresh fish can be seen in the more prolific rivers of the east coast. A fisherman has just hooked a good fish in a shallow pool on a greased line and is waiting for him to settle down before getting out on to the bank to play him (*G. L. Carlisle*)

and line is perfectly suitable for this type of fishing. Indeed, in very low, clear water, when using tiny flies and casts of trout thicknesses, a 12ft rod is too powerful to allow of the playing, and especially hooking, of salmon without many breaks. A trout rod is then obligatory. But these are exceptional circumstances.

THE REEL

The reel must be big enough to hold the line and 80–100yd of backing, and should have the very lightest of checks or ratchets. In design it should preferably be of the deep, narrow drum type because a quick recovery of the line is often vital in this form of fishing. In theory, a multiplying reel is ideal.

EXTRAS

Two other minor accessories will be found useful. These are a thermometer in a metal case and a pair of polarized glasses. It is sometimes essential that the temperatures of the water and air be known, and much added pleasure can be derived from fishing in low, clear water when every movement of the fish and the fly can be noted with the aid of the polarized lenses.

CHOICE OF FLY

Whereas in sunk-line fishing I would hesitate to attribute more than 5 per cent of one's success to judgment in choosing the right fly to fish with (provided always that it is the right size), and would suggest that 95 per cent was derived from the skill with which it was fished, in greased-line fishing matters are very different. Probably as much as 50 per cent of one's luck depends on using the right size and pattern of fly in the right place.

Flies, therefore, form a subject of the greatest importance, and before any attempt is made to define the successful methods of presenting them a thorough understanding of the principles governing the choice of a fly at any particular time and place is essential.

What the small fly represents to the salmon no one knows. There are probably as many theories about this as there are anglers. The facts are that as soon as the water temperature rises above 48°F the salmon undergoes a fundamental change in behaviour. He no longer rests on the bottom in deep water and allows his thoughts to become concentrated on the aqueous life immediately surrounding him. He moves into shallower water, tends to lie on top of rather than behind obstructions, and concentrates his attention on the surface and the immediate sub-surface of the river.

More important still is that fact that now an object representing a small fish of about 3in in length and swimming at some depth in the water apparently ceases to interest him. I went to look at some salmon fry which were being reared in a tank at Aberdeen University since this was written. They were fed with daphnia (a form of water flea) which were shaken into the tank from above. As soon as they were into the water the fry came up to the surface and started to eat them. The most remarkable thing, however, was that the fish, at whatever level they happened to be in the tank, ceased to take any notice of the daphnia which were on their own level or below them, and would even swim about looking upwards for more food which, if given them, they would immediately seize, but would not take the food which swam almost into their mouths. Only about one-quarter of the daphnia were consumed, the remainder floating down and settling on or near the floor of the tank on to which the fry again settled when no more daphnia were forthcoming. Even now, though left until very hungry and though surrounded with scores of living morsels of food, they refused to look at them unless, as occasionally happened, an odd daphnia swam up towards the surface. But a much smaller object of about 1in in length, moving very near to the surface, attracts his immediate attention and reawakens some half-forgotten instinct to chase and seize. I am reasonably sure that all our greased-line flies are far too small.

Flies for greased-line fishing fall into two categories. The first is the long, thinly dressed type, usually known as the low-water dressing. The second is the short, rather more solidly dressed, fly often tied on double hooks. There are, naturally, advantages in each not possessed by the other and it would be a mistake to dogmatize over the matter of choice. Both have their time and place in normal fishing.

On the question of the sizes required there is, however— fortunately—little argument. It is generally agreed that the complete greased-line angler is equipped with flies ranging in size from No 4 down to No 10, that is, from $\frac{15}{16}$in to $\frac{9}{16}$in in overall length of dressing. But where the low-water dressed type of fly is used, the length of the hook and shank will exceed this by over 25 per cent. (A low-water hook for a No 4 fly measures $1\frac{1}{4}$in and for a No 10 nearly $\frac{3}{4}$in.)

On the question of pattern there are two schools of thought. The first takes the view that pattern has no influence whatever on the effectiveness of a fly. However, it is noticeable that, while plenty of this school will be met who will argue hotly over the absurdity of supposing that patterns or colour matter to the fish, I have yet to encounter one of them who does not keep his fly-box crammed with an assortment of a number of different patterns, and who changes from one to another just as often as the protagonist of the opposite school who believes that the dictum 'a bright fly for a bright day' etc, is as true for greased line as for sunk-line fishing.

I firmly believe that colour, or rather tone, is every bit as important in the selection of the correct greased-line fly as in the case of the sunk fly; and that the same principles exactly govern the choice at any moment, and for the same reasons as given in chapter 4 (see page 59).

How many patterns you carry with you will depend largely

on your own temperament. You may feel that conditions of light and river clarity should be divided into seven or eight stages each requiring a different tone of fly. In this case you will require as many patterns. You may, on the other hand, say with Mr Wood that there are only two conditions, bright and dull, and that therefore two patterns are sufficient. For myself, I prefer to have four patterns and divide the light variations into four stages, each with its own fly.

1 Very bright—Silver-Blue
2 Bright—Logie
3 Normal—Blue Charm
4 Dull—Thunder and Lightning

It will be noted that, with the exception of the Thunder and Lightning, all these flies are essentially blue in colour. This is as it should be since normally the greased line is fished in clear water in which blue light penetrates readily.

It is the clarity of the water which chiefly determines my choice of pattern. If the river is coloured I am inclined to use the Thunder and Lightning at all times, but if it is a very bright day, I may use the Logie with its red and yellow body in its place.

The important thing to remember, however, is that whatever your personal fancy in the matter of patterns, however many you feel you must have, it is essential that each pattern be carried in the complete range of sizes. This is largely for a psychological reason. You may hook or rise a fish on, say, a Silver-Blue. You may feel that the fly might be more successful if it were smaller. But if you do not happen to have a smaller size of this pattern you will be very loath to discard your Silver-Blue, which has given results, for another fly of the right size which you feel may not be so good.

I think, too, that unless you possess the full range of sizes of each pattern of your choice, tied on both the long- and the short-shanked types of hook, you will often feel, and probably with reason, that your equipment is not complete.

CHOICE OF CAST

There are three golden rules to be observed in the choice of cast:

1 Use the finest gut you dare to fish with. In a heavy river like the Spey or the Blackwater or Shannon you cannot use very fine gut or you will get broken every time a fish crosses the stream. But in rivers like the Dee or the Bann, you can fish, except in high water, with fuse gut with safety. With small flies there is no doubt whatever that gut shows up relatively like a cable, and the sight of it does not induce a fish to take readily. I have found that the finer the cast, the more fish I hook. The limiting factor is arrived at when the number of fish by which you are broken in play on fine casts exceeds the number you have failed to hook because the cast is heavy. Only experience can decide this for the individual.

2 Use a cast of 3yd in length, and never vary from this. On the length of your cast will depend, to a great extent, the depth at which your fly fishes. The longer the cast the deeper will the fly sink. It is most important that this item should remain constant since a major part of the reason for changing your fly size will often be to ensure the correct depth for the fly.

3 Handle the cast as little as possible, especially with greasy fingers. Nylon casts, which everyone uses nowadays, are difficult to clean and float too easily. The best way to clean a cast is with a rag soaked in carbon tetra-chloride.

6

Presentation

Two beliefs about greased-line fishing in general are commonly held. The first is that it requires superlative skill to fish it well, the second that all sorts of tricks of technique must be learnt before this skill can be gained.

Let me hasten to disillusion you. It requires nowhere near the same measure of skill to catch salmon on the greased line as with the sunk fly.

It is on the manner of presentation of the correctly chosen fly that success or failure to catch fish will primarily depend. On both the choice of fly and on the manner of its presentation there has been much muddled thinking and a regrettable amount of nonsense written. The result is that a large proportion of fishermen using this method have no true idea of what they are doing or why.

CHOICE OF FLY

The choice of fly is the first problem that faces the angler on arrival at his pool. With pattern and colour he is on fairly safe ground. It is a normal late spring day, the river is clear and of normal height. He decides to start with a Blue Charm. What size shall he use?

Mr Wood once wrote 'the basic size is a No 6'. These are golden words which should never be forgotten. They are

80

golden not because they are necessarily true, but because they will tend to prevent the most common of all faults seen in greased-line fishing—using a fly which is unnecessarily small.

We have supposed, as a basis on which the size of a fly will be chosen, that in warm water the fish will be expecting a smaller prey than in cooler water. The thermometer must therefore be the first guide. We can create a table giving the sizes of fly suitable for each temperature.

Temperature (°F)	Size
48–50	No 4
50–52	No 5
52–54	No 6
54–56	No 7
56–58	No 8
58–60	No 9
60 and above	No 10

This, however, is merely the framework on which the choice is founded. Three other factors modify this choice. These are:

1 *Average Speed of Current* This refers essentially only to that part of the pool being fished at the moment. By average speed is meant the speed in that part of the arc of water being fished in which the expectation of catching a fish is highest. This will normally be half-way both in distance and in speed of flow of the current between the beginning and the end of the cast. If this is very fast, a fly two sizes larger should be used. If fast, a size larger, if slower than normal one size smaller, and if very slow, two sizes smaller.

2 *Height of the River* This, in a sense, is often another way of saying the same thing as in the previous paragraph. But it calls attention to the fact that when the river rises not only does it become bigger, but also faster. This increase in speed very often passes unnoticed, and on going to a pool which has been fished successfully with a No 7 the previous day and finding it 3–4in higher (in fast rivers this rise actually almost doubles the volume of the water), it is not always apparent

that the current now runs throughout very much more rapidly. Consequently for a rise of 2–3in it is necessary to increase the size of the fly by one; for a fall of the same amount the size of the fly should, of course, be likewise decreased. For greater rises and falls than this, two or even three sizes of difference should be used.

3 *Colour of Water* In a coloured water the fisherman can afford to use a size larger than in clear water. In very coloured water this can be increased to two sizes.

My friend the late J. B. Rosher, who was a most experienced greased-line fisherman, had an excellent points system for estimating the correct size of fly. Its great virtue lay, to my mind, not in its exactitude, but in the confidence which it gave to his fishing. He was unshakable in his belief that his choice of fly could not be bettered.

He started with the basic temperature-size table that I have given, and each size of fly was numbered in points, ie a No 6 was worth 6 points. Consequently a water temperature of 52–54°F became worth 6 points. He now added or subtracted points for the reasons indicated in the previous paragraphs.

His reasoning went like this:

		Points
Temperature	53°F	6
Speed of current	very fast	− 2
Height of river	3in below normal	+ 1
Colour of water	clear	0
	Result	5

A No 5 was therefore the right size—and so it usually proved to be.

The beauty of this method is that constant attention to detail is required. For instance, every hour or so on a warm day, into the water goes the thermometer. By 11 o'clock the sun has raised the temperature from 53°F to 55°F. So one point is added and the fly changed from a 5 to a 6. If it rises to 58°F in mid-afternoon and he is fishing the same piece of water again, the fly he now uses is a 7.

It would be overstating the case to suggest that this system is foolproof. It cannot be any more than any other rule of thumb system. But it is by far the best basis for the choice of size of fly which I have ever encountered, and I have no hesitation in recommending it to all my fellow fishermen.

PRESENTATION

The next problem that arises is that of presenting this now correctly chosen fly to the fish. On this I find myself at variance with most of the experts, and before putting forward what I consider to be a correct way of fishing the small fly, it behoves me to explain why I am not in agreement with most others.

The greased-line method was invented by Mr Wood some forty-five years ago, and has been based ever since on the results of Mr Wood's own observations and practice, and of those who follow him as closely as possible. Now, as I have written elsewhere, Cairnton, the beat of which Mr Wood was tenant for so many years, has certain peculiarities which make it most untypical of a beat on a normal salmon river. Further, Mr Wood was not, apart from his Cairnton days, in any sense an experienced fisherman. But he was a highly intelligent observer, and finding himself, a comparative novice, the tenant of this singular beat, he evolved a method of fishing it which was ideally suited to Cairnton, but quite unsuitable to almost any other beat. I have, for instance, already pointed out the fallacy of imagining that a 12ft rod can be fished single-handed for a whole day in ordinary pools.

Ever since then every work that Mr Wood has written, every opinion he has ever expressed, has been taken as gospel truth, and most of the greased-line fishing seen today is more or less an exact copy of the methods advocated by its founder, who fished it virtually only on his own very singular water.

The point of technique with which I disagree most violently is that of the method of presentation of the fly. Let us revert for a moment to first principles and see just what it is that we are trying to do when fishing the small fly on the greased line. Essentially we are tempting a salmon to attack a small creature swimming near the surface. We must analyse this more closely.

'A small creature'—what precisely do we mean? How small? Why does it vary in size? It has already been stated that to imagine that the natural summer sea food of the salmon is the leptocephalus of the eel which varies in size according to the temperature of the water in which it is found, gives an excellent working theory upon which to base one's fishing. But useful and attractive as it may be to have such a cut-and-dried hypothesis to explain why a No 7 is better than a No 6 fly under certain circumstances, and correct though it may be in principle, it seems to me at one moment far too exact, at another far too inexact in detail.

For example, the range in size of the leptocephalus is from about $\frac{2}{5}$in off the Bermudas to $2\frac{1}{2}$in at the point of entry of the North Atlantic Drift into the North Sea. The range of temperature of the Gulf Stream and North Atlantic Drift between these two points is from about 68°F down to about 50°F. The two scales do not agree. We ought, on this reckoning, to be using flies of 2–$2\frac{1}{2}$in in water temperatures of 48–55°F, instead of the 1in flies which have been found by experience to be successful.

Now it may well be that the sizes of flies which we use are indeed not correct—and I have more than a suspicion that this is so. (This question will be discussed in a later chapter.) For the moment we are concerned with the method of fishing with the normal range of flies and in discovering why it is that changes of as little as $\frac{1}{16}$in in the size of our flies can make so much difference to the reaction of the salmon towards them.

River Shannon at Limerick (*G. L. Carlisle*)

Why do we change from a No 6 to a No 7 when the temperature rises by 2°F?

I think the answer is that temperature, as a direct influence, is not the cause. The truth is that changes in temperature during the period when the greased line is normally fished are associated nine times out of ten with variations in the height and, consequently, speed of flow of the river.

Allied to this must be taken into account the general tendency of fish to move up into faster-flowing water as the day progresses and the river warms. This is a natural reaction to the de-oxygenation of its atmosphere induced by a rising temperature of a creature which breathes through water and whose metabolic rate also rises with increases of temperature.

The net result is that it is perfectly defensible to argue that rises in temperature have in themselves no effect upon the sizes of flies we should use, but that it is the changes in the speed of flow of the water over the fish that induce these variations in size. And I believe this to be a basically sound and correct argument. It is, for example, difficult to explain the following circumstance in any other way. On, let us say, 10 May this year, I shall probably be using a No 5 or No 6 fly before noon on my Garry beat. At the same moment one of my friends will be using a No 7 on a similarly placed beat of the Dee, while another will probably be using a No 8 or 9 on a beat of the Don. The anomaly, I say, is explained by the fact that the Garry is a faster river than the Dee throughout, and the Dee in turn is faster than the Don, and more particularly, that the Garry fish lie in faster-flowing streams than those of the Dee—and so on. 'But why', you will ask, 'does the speed of the current have this effect on the size of the fly?'

In our analysis we have dealt with the words 'a small creature'. The next word is 'swimming', and it is this word which gives the key to the answer. This creature, your fly, must give the illusion of swimming under its own power.

I have already, when discussing the presentation of the

sunk fly, emphasized that there is a natural relationship between the size of a fish or an aquatic animal and the natural
speed at which it can and does swim. The minnow cannot
swim at the same speed as the salmon for the very good
reason that its energy/surface ratio cannot be as great. Likewise a creature of $\frac{1}{2}$in in length cannot swim at the speed of a
3in minnow. If, therefore, you are to create an illusion of an
animal of the size of a No 7 fly ($\frac{3}{4}$in) swimming, it must go
through the water at a speed at which a creature of this size
could swim.

Those who have kept aquaria will doubtless have owned a
few specimens of the tiny Goby, or of the Millions Fish
(*Lebistes*). Using these last as guinea-pigs I have attempted
to compute the sort of speed at which they swim in still water.
The male *Lebistes* which is about 1in in length can make a
dart into cover at about 5mph, but when harried round the
aquarium and made to swim several yards, it does little better
than $2\frac{1}{2}$mph. The cruising speed is not more than $1\frac{1}{2}$mph. The
figures for the female, which is nearly double the length, are
about half as great again.

If the 1in fly represents a fish, these figures will approximate
to the speeds at which such a fish can and does swim. If,
however, it represents a crustacean like the shrimp, then the
speeds given are at least twice what they should be; and if the
leptocephalus, then the figures must be rather more than
halved again. And when the fly is reduced in size from a
No 6 to a No 10, the speed at which it moves through the
water must equally be reduced by nearly half if it is to create
the proper illusion.

In the exercise of our art as fishermen the variations in
the speeds at which the fly can be fished are limited to variations in the lateral component of the total water speed of
the fly (ie we cannot alter the speed of the current and if the
fly is held stationary, it must have a water speed equal to this.
But we can reduce the increase in speed induced by our fly

moving sideways across the current by fishing it very slowly).
This variation may not, however, be sufficient so we do the
next best thing. We put on a bigger fly which represents a
bigger fish or animal, and which has therefore a greater
natural speed of swimming.

The reader may now ask with reason, 'Why then do we not
always use the larger sizes of fly? Surely this would give
greater latitude for errors in technique?'. 'Absolutely true', I
answer, 'but owing to the manner in which our flies are
constructed, the use of a bigger fly in slow-swimming currents
produces disillusionment of an even more serious character
than excessive speed of movement. Such a fly, due to the
weight of its hook, falls off the horizontal axis. It ceases to
swim through the water quite parallel to the surface but does
so pointing upwards to it.'

Now is the moment to consider the only radical change in
design which has been made in salmon flies since fly-fishing
first began. I refer to the long shank low-water hook and
dressing. This type of fly was designed for three reasons.
First, it was felt that the type of fly in general use was too
heavily dressed. Second, it was believed that to place the
hook well behind the body of the fly would increase the
angler's chances of catching those fish which come short.
Third, that a bigger hook would give a more secure hold once
the fish was on. This type of fly has proved a tremendous
success—but, I submit, not for any of the reasons for which
it was initially designed.

This type of fly is successful because:
1 It is lightly dressed. Leaving aside any visual quality that
a thin dressing may have, its mechanical effect is marked.
A thin sketchy wing and hackle attached to the throat of a
fly offers less resistance and has considerably less tendency to
buoy the fore-end of the fly up in the water. This type of fly
is, on this account, likely to swim horizontally more easily
than heavily dressed flies.

2   The iron of the hook is of lighter and finer metal than normal hooks of the same length. A No 6 low-water hook is of the same length as a No 4 Dee hook or a No 2 of any other pattern. But it is made of wire of the same gauge as a No 6 of the Dee or other patterns. It has, therefore, a larger surface / weight ratio and swims or fishes nearer to the surface than the same length of fly with heavier gauge hooks.

3   It does, in fact, give a bigger lure than its size number indicates. Simply because the dressing is shorter does not, to my way of thinking, alter the size of the fly. It must be looked at as a whole, and the shank and hook are an integral part of a complete fly. It is well known that completely bare hooks will, on occasion, catch salmon. To suppose that the fish only sees the thinly dressed body of a No 6 low-water fly and ignores the shank and hook behind the dressing, which has very little less bulk than that of the dressed portion, is to me an illogical view. I believe that the main reason why these low-water dressed flies are so successful is because they are, in fact, bigger flies which do not suffer from the disadvantages of the standard type of bigger flies.

'Why, then', you will ask, 'do we not always use low-water dressed flies with long shanks?'

The answer is that, though being lightly dressed and therefore not so liable to fall into a vertical position as if heavily dressed, they are none the less more liable to this failing than shorter-shanked flies would be. The turning moment about the point of support, the eye, is greater because the shank is longer. Added to this is the fact that whereas in a short, fat fly, a slight deviation from the horizontal is not very noticeable, the same deviation in the case of a long, thin fly immediately catches the eye. In the first instance the wing is the fly, in the latter the shank is the fly. Long-shanked low-water flies cannot therefore be used successfully in slow-running water. But they are excellent in fast streams. In my view, they are, paradoxically, best for general use in a higher water than in low water.

7

Fishing the Fly

There is a military convention that when orders are being issued the commander himself shall write the intention paragraph detailing the general principles of the operation he intends his formation to engage in. The idea behind this is twofold. There must be no doubt as to what the commander's intention really is, and, should anything now happen to him, his trained staff or his intelligent subordinates can carry on and make a satisfactory plan of their own. It is significant that the intention paragraph always comes after the preamble giving information about 'the enemy and own troops', but before the plan.

I feel now somewhat as a general must feel who has just written his intention paragraph. The information is given, the intention clear. If a competent fisherman, but one who had never heard of greased-line fishing before, were to read what is so far written about it he should soon, if I have expressed myself clearly, be able, with a little thought, to fish a beat as well as the practised expert.

Certain details may, however, need further classification. The first of them relates to the angle at which the small fly should be cast. My novice would be in no doubt about this. 'The fly must be fished slowly', he would say to himself, 'so it is obvious that the longer the line I can throw, and the more downstream I can throw it, the more slowly I can fish my fly while, at the same time, covering my fish.' And I say he would be right.

But this is not, if you believe many of the textbooks, the current way of fishing the greased line. Mr Wood wrote, 'In broken water, I cast rather more upstream than the orthodox cast of a salmon fisherman', and also 'I find the best angle to present the fly is that which shows it broadside to the fish.' These statements, either together or alone, have in the course of time, suffered distortion. It is no unusual occurrence to see a man fishing the greased line upstream in the manner of a dry fly. When comment is made the answer usually comes out pat, 'But Wood said you should fish upstream!'.

This, I hope, is not what Wood intended. What he wrote, and intended to imply, was that he cast more squarely across than would be considered normal, but compensated for possible drag by mending his line quickly and often. Arthur Wood essentially believed in the necessity of fishing the small fly slowly. 'Ordinarily I fish as slowly as possible, and the late Ernest Crosfield often made the remark that each of my casts took two or three times as long as any other he had seen', he wrote to W. J. Barry. And he reiterates the same argument over and over again. Why, then, if he wanted to fish his fly as slowly as possible did he cast more squarely across the stream than normal?

The answer is clear to me. He liked to fish with a single-handed rod and a light line, he disliked wading and preferred to fish from the bank. Except by casting square across the river there was no other way in which he could get the distance which he wanted. This, I say, is a thoroughly bad way to fish and is, in my view, only a last resort. It is asking for rises from fish which do not take, because however carefully one mends the line, drag cannot be eliminated entirely. Of these Wood had, on his own admission, far more than his proper share. That he usually got the fish in the end is a reflection rather

91

River Shannon—upper reaches. This magnificent river was at one
time one of the greatest and most prolific salmon rivers in the world.
Hydro-electric schemes, over-netting and pollution reduced it to medi-
ocrity during the early half of the century, but by taking protective
measures the Irish government has largely restored the Shannon and
it should continue to improve. The boat being used is known as a cot
and is of a type peculiar to this river, fast and easy to row or pole but
very unstable to fish from (*the late C. V. Hancock*)

on his refusal to admit defeat than on his method of fishing.

It is quite illogical to adopt the technique of a man who fished, because he preferred to, in what you or I might describe as a makeshift manner on a beat which might purposely have been designed for such a manner of fishing, when there are better ways of achieving the same end. Forget all this upstream business. Get as close to your fish as you can by wading, throw as long a line as you can manage, and as much downstream as you can. This is the easiest and best way of fishing your fly slowly and at a natural swimming angle over the fish.

Notwithstanding this, however, the question of presenting the fly 'broadside to the fish' is not so easily explained. By broadside it is presumed that broadside to the axis on which the fish is lying is meant. For the whole sentence of which I have already quoted the first part runs, 'I find the best angle to present the fly is that which shows it broadside to the fish; the latter invariably comes some yards to meet the fly, which is taken by it across its mouth.' (cf The Lonsdale Library, *Salmon Fishing*, p248.)

Now there is only one way in which a fly can be presented broadside to a fish without a drag, and that is if it is drifting almost unchecked, downstream.

Picture to yourself, now, what really happens. In a strong stream in the middle of the river is lying a taking fish. But it is too far away to be reached with a downstream cast which fishes the fly slowly over him. It can just be reached with a long square cast. This is made, and a mend immediately placed upstream. Until this mend has straightened out the fly will drift unchecked downstream. As the line tightens, however, the fly is given a tiny drag across the stream, but at once another mend upstream is made. The fly now drifts again.

What, during these operations, is the speed of the fly? Its bank speed is the same as that of the current, but its water speed is practically nothing. This fly is fishing just about as slowly as is possible because the creature which it represents would, if following the same path, be swimming very slowly indeed. And while you may not immediately realize this, the salmon certainly does.

Here, then, is the secret of this square casting. In very strong streams it is often the only way in which a fish can reasonably be caught, since even hanging the fly immobile (relative to yourself) may not lower its water speed sufficiently. But to keep the fly from dragging, constant and exaggerated mends are required. This is tiresome, difficult to accomplish without moving the fly too much, and usually unnecessarily laborious in normal streams when other easier ways exist. Nor do I believe that broadside is the best angle at which to present the fly to the fish. However, if you do fish in this particular style it is the only way you can present it. But it cannot be an optimum. I have stated that 48°F is the critical water temperature. Below this the sunk fly should be used; above it, the greased line. The pin-pointing of this temperature at so exact a figure is the result of experience, and I do not think that many will be found to disagree with it.

But there is a large school of thought which believes that when the air is colder than the water it is useless to fish the greased line, and which reverts either to the big fly or, more often, to the bait under such conditions. I have always attempted, without success, to discover the argument upon which this proposition is founded.

I agree wholeheartedly with the dictum that when the air is colder than the water, fishing conditions are very poor. And they are poor for a perfectly logical and, to me, obvious reason. This is that the water is tending to be cooled rather rapidly. At normal fishing temperatures, ie up to 60°F, this condition can never be other than harmful to fishing prospects for the reasons that firstly, cooling water means a lowering in temperature of the fish itself with a consequent slowing up of its reflexes and metabolism; secondly, lowering of water temperature means an automatic lowering of the quantity of oxygen dissolved in the water which is available to the fish. While this cooling process continues, the burning up of oxygen for energy to be dissipated in such frivolous occupations as seizing flies is the one thing the fish must avoid. Its atmosphere is a matter of constant anxiety to the fish and a shortage of oxygen is a permanent threat which hangs over his head like the sword of Damocles. In parenthesis, this is the reason why an east wind, a frosty evening, an air temperature which fails to rise in the morning, in short, anything which tends to cool the water below its existing temperature, makes for bad fishing.

When the air is cooler than the water is, we must accept the fact of as poor a condition for greased-line fishing as it is possible to have. But it is equally poor for any other form of legitimate fishing. If the water temperature remains, however, about 48°F, the salmon are still surface-minded, and I have no hesitation in saying that, slight though your chances may be with the greased line, they are infinitely better than with any other method. If you believe that this condition denies all hope with the floating line, then the sensible thing to do is to stop fishing and wait for an improvement. To fish the sunk fly is probably a waste of time and energy, as it is to use the greased line at water temperature of less than 48°F.

I cannot leave this chapter without referring to a point which crops up every year and results, in my view, not only in greatly reduced bags, but also often in the use of the bait by otherwise confirmed fly-fishermen. This is what I call the greased-line complex. By this I mean the determination shown by a number of fishermen to use the greased line too early in the season.

The decision as to the right moment to change from the sunk fly to the greased line is often a difficult one. For the visiting angler any empirical formula fails because the data obtainable are always incomplete. An analysis of the factors which determine the solution of the problem will give an indication of the difficulties.

It is emphatically true to say that at any water temperature under 48°F the sunk fly will always beat the greased line. It will usually do so at temperatures below 50°F, and often below 52°F. But, and this is a big but, we must recognize that in fishing with the small greased-line fly we are tacitly acknowledging a complete change of behaviour and outlook in the fish. The salmon is now looking at the surface where before his attention was fixed in the deeper strata. So fundamental a change of behaviour is not ephemeral. Once accomplished it is virtually permanent for the season. It is not, therefore, engendered by minor and fleeting rises of temperature above the critical point. It requires a permanent rise over several days and nights before the greased-line complex is fixed in the salmon.

Information as to temperatures throughout the twenty-four hours is not usually available to the newly arrived angler. He may, on a warm April morning, take the water temperature and find it 49°F. It may rise to 52°F in mid-afternoon and fall back to 49°F when he leaves the river at 6 p.m. But the previous day it may never have attained 46°F, and it will fall to below this figure for the greater part of a still, long night. Under such circumstances the sunk fly will, I say, always, always beat the greased line. Season after season I see brother anglers leaving after a fortnight's fishing in March, April and even early May, with bags sometimes but a tenth of what they should have been because they would insist on using the greased line far too early in the year.

MENDING

It may have come to the notice of the reader that very little in this book is said upon the subject of mending. There is a reason for this. I am quite satisfied that mending becomes a vice with most fishermen, and that they use this trick not only far too much, but even to the detriment of their own fishing. Let me put my argument very briefly. Casting square, even upstream, is successful only in certain very specialized pools, or sometimes under conditions of very low, warm water. Its effect is to create drag, and mend as often as you will, it is impossible to fish the fly, when so cast, without drag. In very slow pools this drag is occasionally required to give life to the fly, and mending is merely a trick used to control the amount of drag and limit the speed of the fly to reasonable proportions. But it is a trick which has its own serious disadvantages. First, very few are sufficiently technically expert to mend without jerking the fly; second, the act of lifting the line off and dripping it back on to the water creates considerable disturbance which, when it is remembered that the fish is interested now only in the surface, will seriously distract his attention from a small fly, and may even frighten him away.

The ideal way to fish the greased line is to cast a very long line and at such an angle that mending need scarcely ever be resorted to. To mend in rough, broken water does little harm. To mend in the glassy glide of a fast tail is almost an angling crime. There are many occasions where a pronounced belly in the line is not only desirable but indeed absolutely essential. For example, many deep pools have very fast, narrow streams running through them. The fish lie on the edge of such streams. The best way to fish most of these is to cast over into the backwater at the far side of the stream and allow a pronounced V-shaped belly to form in the line. This has the effect of dragging the fly downstream into the current. The result is that, whereas the fly is moving fast relative to yourself on the bank, its water speed is not nearly so great as you might imagine, since much of its apparent pace would be natural to any object floating freely in the current. I am quite sure that the fish is prepared to regard the fly moving in this manner more favourably than one which is constantly being jerked for short distances and in the interim period being held stationary against a fast stream. I believe the spinning angler who fishes his bait fast downstream had discovered this fact also.

Incidentally, because the floating line casts far more shadow than does the same line submerged, due to the bending of the water surface on which it lies, it often pays, even in high summer, to fish a light sunk line in preference to the greased line, especially in smooth water.

CONTACT

Fish which come to the small fly will sometimes be seen to rise. It has been written, and it is a very commonly held belief, that the rise should always be seen. With this, once more, I disagree entirely. Except in very slack water, if the fly is being correctly fished, the rise of a fish to take it should not be noticeable on the surface. Nearly all attempts which miss the fly completely show as rises, but a very large proportion of plucks and pulls from fish which are not hooked also show as rises. The proportion of fish which take the fly in the proper manner and which show as rises should be very small indeed and should, in theory, be confined to those which take in very slack water. Whenever I hear a man say that he has caught a fish which 'took the fly with a beautiful head and tail rise', I will lay odds that the next thing he says is, 'I also rose two more and pulled yet another', or something of the sort. This convinces me that that man is fishing his fly in an incorrect manner.

River Inver, Sutherland. This is basically a typical spate river, fishing well when there is water and badly when low. But the Inver, in fact, has been partly transformed by some imaginative and very well-executed pool creation which has been a great success. The reason is that unlike some groynes which are built wrongly, ie pointing downstream, these have been placed square across the river and do not create backwaters on either side of the stream (*L. S. Paterson*)

Fishing the Fly

To understand why this statement is made with so much emphasis it is necessary to consider the manner in which the salmon takes the small fly. If you will refer to Chapter 4 of this book you will see what has been said about the way in which a salmon takes the sunk fly. Precisely the same is true of the ways in which he takes the small, barely submerged fly. He does not rise and go down with it in the manner of a trout. He sees it in front and to one side of him, and he swims forward in an effort to intercept it at the moment when it will lie directly ahead of him. He tries as far as possible to remain on an even keel throughout.

If the fish makes a good shot, if he times his forward movement properly, he will arrive with his mouth ready open at a certain point in the water at precisely the same moment as this point is reached by the fly. He will, too, have timed matters so that now he has lost much of his forward movement and is on the point of being carried back again by the stream. There should be no necessity for him either to turn to the side or to plunge forward and downwards with the fly. Whether he succeeds or not in taking with such perfection will depend almost entirely upon how well you, the angler, are fishing your fly.

Most rises which are seen are caused by the fly being fished too fast and, what is often the same thing, with drag. When the fly is dragged it is normally impossible for the fish to make the forward allowance necessary to intercept it with any accuracy in the right place. He is rather in the position of a pheasant shot whose birds suddenly fly through a violent cross-wind just before he shoots. Further, a fly being dragged is pulled to the surface. The object in greasing the line is to fish the fly near the surface, but, as I have postulated in my previous book, *Salmon Fishing, Philosophy and Practice*, not too near.

The result is that the fish is forced to turn to get the fly, and at the same time swims forwards and upwards both

John Ashley Cooper is one of the best and most experienced salmon fishermen in the world. Here he is at Careysville gaffing his own salmon. Note the very long handled gaff, so necessary where there are steep banks, the mittens he wears rather than gloves and the fact that, struck from underneath, the fish will surely tear badly. But the special thing about this picture is that this most expert fisherman has played his fish until it has been lying on its side in quiet shallow water. Now, knowing that the salmon will not move again, he has put his rod down, walked quietly to the fish and gaffed him. His confidence stems from the fact that he has been standing well away from the water's edge while playing the salmon. Many fish are lost by anglers standing too near in the closing stages (*Frank O'Brien*)

farther and faster than he had intended. Born of such causes are, I believe, nine out of ten of all rises seen in fast or normal streams. And I have no hesitation in saying that they are due to faulty technique on the part of the angler.

In slack water, however, rises will usually and very properly be seen. This is because there is not enough pace in the stream to arrest the forward movement of the fish once he has taken hold of the fly. He follows through, therefore, on the same line in which he has come forward and usually breaks the surface in a head and tail rise.

It will be appreciated, therefore, that if you are fishing your fly perfectly you will not, in most cases, receive any visible warning in the shape of a rise to tell you that a fish has taken your fly. The difficulties of hooking him are thus greatly magnified. If you are to rely upon feeling the pull given by the perfect take, you will be far too late to do anything about it, and more likely than not, the fly will have been quietly ejected from the front of his opened mouth as the fish dropped back towards his lie.

But you do receive warning in another manner. The end of the line, which is swinging round, will suddenly be seen to check as the fish takes hold. Immediately this is seen, action calculated to hook the fish must be taken. Occasionally, in very strong water the fish only just reaches the fly and grabs at it as he starts to be carried back by the current. In such cases, nothing will be seen at all before the strong pull of the fish is felt. Here any action on the part of the angler is useless. By the time the pull has registered, the fish is either properly hooked, poorly hooked, or is away.

It is, I hope, unnecessary for me to point out the vital importance to the greased-line angler of watching his line with the utmost attention through every inch of its fishing arc.

It is astonishing how very gentle the effect of so big a fish as a salmon taking the small fly can often be. I have seen competent anglers miss fish after fish through failing to realize that they were being taken and many of them refused to believe that the tiny. draw that was sometimes felt as the fish let go was anything other than a parr.

It should not be necessary either for me to state what the correct action on becoming aware of a fish should be. By realizing how the fish takes and at the same time how your fly is swimming, it should be easy to put two and two together and determine what to do.

Never strike. By offering resistance to the taking fish you are presenting him with the only chance he has of getting rid of the fly. You must do the very reverse. The instant that you become aware that something is stopping your fly you must immediately, somehow or another, produce slack line. The effect you strive now to achieve is to get as big a belly of line as possible lying below the fish so that when he opens his mouth on feeling the pull of the stream (due to this belly) on the fly, it will be drawn backwards and sideways over the corner of his mouth. The only way you can create this belly is by slackening off before the fish begins to drop back, too.

In Fig 7 is shown, in stages, the effect of immediate slackening of the line when the fish takes. In No 1 the fish, still moving forward, but decelerating rapidly, has taken hold of the fly. In No 2, the angler has now realized he has a fish and has let everything go. The fish has come to a standstill, but the belly is forming. In No 3 the fish is starting to fall

Fig 7 Slackening the line

back, but there is a good belly formed behind him and, provided the angler still does nothing, the fish cannot get rid of the fly.

When should the strike be made? The answer is never, never at all; the current does the striking. Suppose, for example, that in No 2 of the diagram the fish has not yet let go of the fly. Suppose it is lying flat in his mouth firmly held between his tongue and palate. Now you strike. The belly is taken up, the fish feels the pull and lets go. Which way is the fly going to go? Obviously straight out of his opened mouth.

When fishing the greased line, especially if you are fishing it well, you cannot ever afford to make anything in the nature of a strike at any time. There is no such thing as leaving a fish too long before tightening up on him.

The importance of acquiring the habit of fishing with a coil of slack held loosely in the free hand will thus be seen. If this habit is adopted and if the rod is always kept in the same plane as the line, the fly will fish round in direct contact with the free hand holding the line and full use can be made of the sensitivity of the finger-tips. It should become an automatic and reflex action on the part of the good greased-line angler to let go immediately the slightest suspicion of a touch or draw is felt on the line, irrespective of whether anything has been seen or not. Many fish which grab the fly in hard streams and which would otherwise be lost will be landed by doing this. The hand is often much quicker than the eye.

Eventually, having taken your time, you will decide to start playing the fish which you know is now hooked. Lift the point of your rod quietly, reel in the few feet or yards of slack line you have given him and, as likely as not, he will be contacted lying quite still, firmly anchored to your fly, in the very place from which he started off.

Precisely the same principles apply to landing a fish with greased-line tackle as with that of the sunk fly. It should not be forgotten, however, that the cast is much finer and weaker and that a drowned line is, in consequence, infinitely more dangerous. Nor should it be forgotten that in low, clear water fish can see very much better than in a river running at early spring levels. Keep well away from him until your fish is ready for the gaff or to be tailed.

8

Bait-Fishing

Much of the early part of this book has been devoted to an examination of the salmon himself, his natural history, his way of life, the reasons for his singular behaviour, and the weaknesses in his mental and physical make-up which must permit us to enjoy any success in fishing him. It is a wonderful thing that we have discovered how to tempt a creature, who does not feed, who cannot eat, into seizing such monstrosities as our flies and baits for reasons which we can never fully understand.

And while fishing with the fly is generally accepted as, and must always remain, the most aesthetically satisfying practice in the art of catching salmon, other more mundane, less mystical methods exist. Fishing with bait, be it minnow, prawn, shrimp or worm, can never, for most salmon fishermen, compare with fly-fishing in the skills and techniques required, nor afford the same thrills in hooking and landing fish. Bait-fishing must always be a second best. But at times even the most confirmed fly-fishermen are compelled to resort to spinning, and for many very keen anglers who have not had the opportunity in their early years to practise with a fly-rod, bait-fishing offers a means, easily learnt with modern tackle, of enjoying successful fishing with less physical effort and requiring less knowledge and technique than is demanded by fly-fishing.

Bait-fishing is an extension of fly-fishing. Almost without exception every good bait-fisherman is also a good fly-fisherman and he fishes his bait with the same reasoning and on the same principles as does the fly-fisherman.

Bait-fishing divides itself naturally into two main types. The first is spinning with minnow, sprat, sand eel, prawn, shrimp or their artificial reproductions. The second is what may be described as bottom fishing for want of a better name. This comprises worm-fishing, either upstream with a single lob-worm or downstream with a bunch of worms, and certain types of prawn fishing.

Before embarking on details of the different methods of bait-fishing it is well to be clear on one or two general points not always realised even by those who fish in no other manner than with the bait.

It is, for instance, propounded that in the early part of the season, or in high water, the bait will always catch more fish than the sunk fly. While the fishing record may confirm this, it is, unmodified, not a true statement of fact. The reasons why it has the appearance of the truth are twofold. First, whereas the competence of most salmon fishermen with the greased line and small fly is generally very high, with the sunk heavy line, big fly and 14–15ft powerful rod it is woefully low and the technique necessary to fish a 3in fly properly is mostly unstudied and unpractised. Secondly, whereas it is certainly true that fish newly entering a beat or pool will take a large bait readily, in general they will not take a fly, which appears smaller and does not sink so deeply, until they have been in the pool for a little time—this may be anything from a few minutes to a day or two. In other words, the fish caught with the bait can also be caught with the fly, but probably has to be left for a while before he will take the fly. And certainly there are a number of fish which will no longer look at the bait but which can be caught with fly. The trouble then is that if no bait-fishing is allowed the same number of fish will be caught with fly only, but they will not probably be caught at the same time as if fished for with a bait.

To confirm this it is only necessary to look at the past and present records of any salmon river which might be termed a fly river. In the Aberdeenshire Dee, for instance, the rod bags have always been about 7,500 fish. In poor years this has dropped to between 4,000 and 5,000. In bumper years it has risen to 8,000–9,000. But whether fished with fly only, as in the days of my youth, or with bait and fly, whether by seventy rods or by twice that number, whether river nets, stake nets or drift nets are said to be killing off all the stock, the average number of rod-caught fish always remains (with the possible exception of the worst of the UDN years) about the same. The answer is that if angler A catches a fish on a golden sprat in pool X on Monday, that fish is not there to be caught either by angler B with a fly on Tuesday nor by angler C in another pool higher up the river a week later. And one of the reasons for the prevalence of bait-fishing is that with most beats nowadays being let on a weekly basis the tenant feels that he must avail himself of the first and every opportunity of catching his fish and cannot afford to leave anything he might catch either for another tenant in the following week, or for another beat higher up the river. For he is quite sure, and with reason, that those fishing lower down are certainly not going to leave anything that can legally be caught on their beat to come up to him.

So, my friend, because time is our enemy and because we are surrounded with greedy and unfriendly neighbours we sometimes feel we have to fish the bait.

9

Spinning for Salmon

The advent of monofil and plaited nylon lines has not only revolutionized the impedimenta of spinning but has made it possible for the complete beginner to acquire sufficient skill in the use of a spinning rod and reel in a few minutes. In the days of Malloch and Silex or Nottingham reels and the rather heavy and clumsy rods required for them, learning to cast a bait accurately and with distance not only needed much practice, but for beginners ensured that much more time was spent on the bank unravelling bird's-nest tangles than in actually fishing. Today all is changed. The tyro has only to go to the tackle shop, tell the assistant what sort of river he is going to fish, buy the outfit recommended, have a practice cast or two on the lawn at home and he is ready for the fray.

Big rivers like the Tay or the Spey require somewhat different spinning tackle from that demanded by small rivers. The Spey fisherman, for instance, requires a rod of 9–11ft and a reel from which he can cast maximum distances. Such a reel can be either of fixed spool type carrying, usually, a monofil line of a breaking strain of 12–18lb or, if greater distances still are desired, revolving drum reels carrying plaited nylon lines of the same strength. The use of the former can be taught to a child in a few minutes. The latter, though said to be foolproof, still require a certain expertise which can be acquired only by practice if over-runs are to be avoided.

For little rivers—even rivers as big as the higher beats of the Aberdeenshire Dee—a single-handed rod of 6–8ft is quite adequate and is more easily used with a fixed spool reel.

En passant, many people imagine that fishing a big river with a spinning-rod is less tiring than with a fly-rod. I have not found this to be the case. Continuously casting a heavy bait long distances is a most wearing exercise and is every bit as tiring as fishing the big fly. And furthermore each individual cast, though there are fewer of them in a given time, requires considerably greater effort.

As with fly-fishing, so with bait-fishing the successful fisherman is he who understands what he is doing and why he is doing it. He fishes a particular bait in a particular manner because his understanding of the fish's reaction at different levels and colour of water to his proffered lures is clear and precise. While fishing his bait the angler must think like the fish and the more keenly he can do so the greater his chances of success.

I do not propose to discuss any further the questions of rods, reels, lines and tackle. These are the prerogative of the tackle-maker and his salesmen. Nor is it necessary to say anything more about how to cast with a bait-rod. Equipped with reasonable tackle, instructed in the mechanical use of it, having checked that any swivels and spinners are functioning satisfactorily, the fisherman is ready to start.

PRESENTING THE BAIT

Of all this gear the only thing of interest to the salmon is the bait. In choosing this the fisherman must, having projected his mind into the fish's way of thinking, make a decision on three basic point. First, what type and size of bait to use, secondly how deep it should be fished, and thirdly, how fast it should be fished. All three are inter-related, all are depen- ·

110

dent on such factors as the season of the year, the temperature and the height of the water, the light, the air temperature and how long the fish have been in the river. And just as the fly-fisherman uses the sunken line and big fly or the greased line and small fly at the appropriate time and under conditions best suited to each, so does the bait-fisherman choose his lure and fish it to suit the conditions prevailing at the time.

But while these factors, these prevailing conditions, may indicate to the fisherman the type of bait he should use and the way he should fish it, they should, to the thinking angler, be regarded as nothing more than a guide. For always he must be trying to keep in the forefront of his mind the actions, thoughts and reactions of the salmon himself. He may think that a 2½in silver Devon looks just right—he likes it. But whether he finds it attractive or not has no bearing on the correctness of his choice. The question he must answer is 'Does the fish like it?', and to answer this he must try to imagine what it is that the fish would be looking for when feeding in the sea in the cool water of a short February day.

Our bait then must conform to what the fish is looking for. It must give the appearance of a fish of at least 3in in length. The modern usage is to fish with artificial baits, wooden or metal Devons, leather eel tails, etc. In the old days we used natural baits such as spratts, silver or golden, sand eels, gudgeon, loach or minnows. These latter, in order to fish at the correct depth, had to be either weighted with lead in their mountings or fished with considerable lead on the cast. They were more trouble to mount, rather more difficult to cast, but, I am quite sure, were more effective as baits than the artificial types. And the reasons for this are first, they were generally bigger, spratts especially; secondly, they were lighter for their size which meant that they could be fished more slowly without sinking and, as a result, thirdly, they did not have to be cast so squarely across the stream in order to give them sufficient speed to prevent them sinking—a speed unnatural to a fish of their size and therefore unrealistic. I emphasize again that with the bait, as with the fly, the task of the angler is to present the lure in such a manner that it represents the natural prey of the salmon behaving in a natural way.

COLOUR

The question of colour, again as with flies, seems relatively unimportant to the salmon—but not, it appears, to the fisherman. Silver, gold, brown, blue, yellow—have your choice, all will catch fish seemingly at random. Most anglers have their own preferences and since brown, gold and yellow are the common choices, more fish, obviously, are caught on lures of these colours than of blue or silver. But just as I, for example, like to use a bright yellow Garry Dog when fishing the greased line, because I can often see it in the water as it fishes, so I rather tend to use a yellowbelly Devon if fishing an artificial, or a golden spratt as a natural bait. But it really does not matter as it seems all the same to a salmon.

DEPTH

The depth at which the bait is fished is, in contrast, of critical importance. How often does one hear the phrase, 'You have to get down to them'? And as a result of the general acceptance of this dictum, how many fishing hours are lost every season in struggles to release baits caught on the bottom, how many good pools ruined for the day by 'otters' sent down the line into the best salmon lies, how many tempers are frayed, how much expensive tackle lost, how many rods weakened or broken?

And as a generalization 'getting down to them' is a false conclusion based on misunderstood premises. The picture on which the dictum is based is of a pool full of salmon all lying dormant on the bottom, all immobile, unobservant, uninterested in anything unless it is, literally, in front of their noses. This is patently nonsense.

112

Salmon seldom lie on the bottom, but usually rest on a stone. They almost never lie behind a stone or rock for the very good reason that they rely on a smooth current without eddies to assist their breathing and to hold them in position. They are never immobile in a stream since they always have to use a swimming motion to a greater or lesser degree to maintain their position (though in still water of a loch they can lie motionless except for their gill cover and mouth movements). Nor, since fish cannot close their eyes, are they ever asleep as we know it.

Furthermore, if fish are awake their lidless eyes are looking. They look towards the surface and see their prey, and perhaps their enemies, from below. Indeed in the summer-time, when the sea is warm and when the small fish, which constitute the salmon's food, are swimming near the surface they are almost certainly seen first as a reflection on the undersurface of the water which disappears as the hunting salmon approaches, leaving the real prey to be seized. While this potted description of the feeding and hunting habits of the salmon is, consciously or unconsciously, tacitly accepted as forming the basis for the method of fishing the greased line and small fly, it is not generally realized that precisely the same considerations govern—or should govern—the ways in which the bait is fished.

In the early months of the season, when the river may be expected to be running full and cold, salmon tend to lie in deeper and slower-flowing parts of the pool. But they still lie on rocks and beside ledges. They do not lie on the bottom. And at all times they are looking towards the surface and are fully aware of what is going on above them.

Of course your bait must be fished deep. But this is a relative term. If it is fished so deep that it is literally scraping the bottom, then it is of no interest, at any rate as food, to the salmon. If, on the other hand, it is fished so near the surface that the fish sees its reflection, brightly lit, which disappears just when it is getting close enough to be interesting, then the salmon, to whom the conservation of his store of energy is of prime importance, may well consider that the seizing of a much less attractive object, the bait itself, requiring much effort to obtain, is not worth leaving his comfortable lodge to acquire.

Deep is, as we have said, a relative term. Many fishermen imagine that their weighted bait is swimming some 10–12ft below the surface. This, unless the bait is cast upstream and allowed to sink without winding in, is quite impossible in any river in which there is a stream in the pools. Fishing deep, even when casting square across the stream, can seldom mean that the bait swims at more than between 3ft and 4ft below the surface and an average would be nearer to 3ft than 4ft. If the angler, by upstream casting, or by overweighting his bait attempts to fish it deeper than this, he will spend more time releasing it from snags than in fishing and as much money again as his fishing rent in replacing lost and broken tackle.

ANGLE TO THE STREAM

The angle to the stream at which a bait should be cast is the subject of much discussion. Modern casting reels and monofil lines allow greater distances to be achieved than were ever possible with such reels as the Silex or Malloch which carried plaited silk lines. In big rivers it is the fashion today to cast very square as far over the stream as possible. That this is a highly successful way of fishing is evinced by the fact that a great number of fish are hooked shortly after the bait has hit the water and before it has had time to sink. When this happens the bait is, in fact, travelling downstream scarcely checked by the tension on the line and, though in a river whose stream may be running at 8–10 mph the bank speed of the bait may seem excessive, to the fish who is only concerned with the bait's water speed, there is nothing unnatural in its

Here is another well known fisherman, Arthur Oglesby, playing a fish in a Dee pool in March when the river is running high and coloured. He is quite relaxed, quite confident that his spinning bait has a good hold, and will land his fish without further shortening his line by stepping backwards and drawing the salmon into the little bay to the left of his stance where he will probably tail it (*Arthur Oglesby*)

movement. The same cast made with the much thicker line used on, say, a Silex reel, would have produced an immediate drag on the bait and destroyed any illusion that it was a small fish swimming at a normal speed.

The thin monofil line has also allowed much lighter baits to be used than in the old days. This line, offering so much less resistance to the stream, allows a light bait to sink deeper without being dragged across the stream to anything like the same extent as when a thicker plaited line is used. But it is my firm impression that, because these lightweight baits can be cast, many fishermen are inclined to use smaller baits than should be fished. Just as I am sure that when fishing the sunk fly nothing smaller than 8/0 should ever be used, so no bait smaller than 3in should ever be fished in the spring months and if 4in and even 5in minnows and spratts were tried they would, as I have already said, be even more successful.

A big, dirty river will often bring forth from that oracle, your gillie, the remark 'You should try a spoon—they'll see it better'. I would contest this. In my experience the spoon— and I prefer the long Norwegian type—is taken most readily when fish are running and particularly if they are fresh fish and in a very clear, cold river. In the springtime, big spoons, much bigger baits than the spinners, and at least 4in in length are obligatory. And because they are big and heavy they have to be, and can afford to be, fished fast. In clear water they can easily be seen by the fish, but in dirty water they tend to fish so fast that, by the time the salmon can see them, they are moving out of his reach.

If you feel that a spoon might attract a fish in spite of dirty water it is better to use a large Mepp, which can be fished even more slowly than a spinning bait. And even if you cannot catch a salmon with it you may very well take a large cannibal brown trout who appear to love them.

10

Spinning in Summer

Fishing the bait in late spring and summer follows the principles set out for fly-fishing. Just as at a given date salmon cease to be interested in the big sunk-line fly and will only take the small fly, so at the same time, mid-April in general, do they become interested only in a much smaller bait than those of the early spring. Summer bait-fishing falls under two headings. First, in clear water when the river runs at summer levels and secondly, in higher water when the river runs in a dirty summer spate.

Fishing a spinning bait in low, clear water is seldom as successful as fishing the fly, save in exceptional rivers, and it is becoming, I am happy to say, the practice among riparian owners on most of our good salmon rivers to forbid all bait-fishing from about mid-April onwards unless the river is in spate. Nevertheless, there are certain rivers, usually small, often the tributaries of major salmon rivers, which run fast and in which the pools tend to form in deep rocky holes which give rise to backwaters which make them either impossible to fish with a fly, or so difficult as to be scarcely worth the trouble. Usually, such rivers are very clear, have a clear and stony bottom, and allow the fish to be seen very easily in the pools with the aid of polarized glasses. Fishing with a small spinning-rod and light tackle is not only very amusing but often very rewarding. A few days so spent will teach the angler more about how salmon behave than almost any other ways of observing them—save only fishing the worm.

For many years I was tenant of one of the best beats of such a river, the Aven, the main tributary of the Spey. It took me two seasons to learn the special techniques required to catch fish, and, but for the expert tuition from the greatest all-round salmon fisherman I have ever seen, Duncan MacNiven, who owned a hotel in Tomintoul, I doubt if ever I would have acquired the necessary skills. He could virtually always catch fish in the Aven if they were in the pools. But for even the most expert and experienced fisherman who did not know the very exact techniques required to catch salmon in a river of this sort, unless the water was big and coloured, success was nearly impossible.

The small baits, never more than 2in, had not only to spin perfectly, but had to be cast with extreme accuracy into slack water on the other side of the stream. Since they could be seen by the fish through the gin-clear water for 20ft or more it was essential that they should never be allowed either to lose natural speed nor to travel with too much water speed. They had to be fished near to the surface and were, in fact, spinning replicas of the greased-line fly and had to behave as nearly as possible as would the small fly.

Salmon taking such a bait could be observed to move forward and upwards and to fall back towards his lie with the bait in his mouth. Watching the fish with polarized glasses there was always a temptation to strike since there was a time-lag between seeing the fish seize the bait and feeling the pull on the line. To strike was usually fatal. The fish, as with fly-fishing, had to be allowed time to hook himself. Often if the bait was incorrectly fished, too fast or too slowly, too deep or too near the surface, a fish would follow the bait right up to the angler's feet. Provided he did not notice the angler and provided the bait was not snatched away from him, this fish could usually be caught when a cast was subsequently fished correctly.

Often in very low water, salmon can be caught by casting nearly directly upstream and fishing the bait at what seems to the angler an impossible speed straight downstream. In reality, of course, this excessive bank speed, when translated into water speed, is quite normal for a small fish swimming with the current.

I cannot emphasize enough the necessity not only of fishing with the utmost care and exactness in such rivers, but also of ensuring that the tackle used is not only fine and delicate, but that such items as the rod and line, the swivels and the bait itself are functioning to perfection.

That I have dwelt on summer spinning in small, clear rivers is by intent. Far too many anglers who wish, for one reason or another, to spin rather than fly-fish in the late spring and summer are content to take out their big rods and use the same tackle and techniques as if fishing in February. That they may make a concession to the season by using a smaller bait does not prevent them from overweighting the cast and fishing the bait along the bottom. In any big river, when conditions for fly-fishing warrant the use of the greased line and small fly, bait-fishing must be conducted on the same lines as on a little, clear stream. Small rods, preferably single-handed, small baits fished near the surface and fine tackle are obligatory. And the greatest success will be achieved by the angler who fishes his bait deliberately to behave as much like the small fly as possible.

With the small baits used it is essential that every item of the equipment must be functioning perfectly. Swivels which do not allow the bait to spin properly, casts which are too heavy, baits which have lost a wing or which move unevenly, will prevent an interested fish from taking.

The golden rule in fishing small summer baits is that they must be small, they must spin properly, and they must be light and be fished very near to the surface. Above all they must always be kept moving at a natural water speed.

Spinning in the dirty water of summer spates, a practice often resorted to by even confirmed fly-fishers, is seldom more rewarding than any other method except worm-fishing. And such chances as it does offer are habitually negatived by an approach which is based on false premises.

'They won't see a small bait in this dirty water', thinks the angler, 'a 3in minnow or a spoon are what's wanted'. And how wrong he is. This is summer, the fish is conditioned to reacting to small flies and baits; the fact that the water is dirty cannot alter this. And just as the fly-fisherman would not dream of using an 8/0 fly at such a time, so the bait-fisherman, if he is to have any chance of success, must persevere with his smaller baits. As a concession to these adverse conditions, he may decide to fish his bait rather more slowly than in normal heights of water. But if it is the wrong size and fished too deep the fish is no more likely to take it in dirty than in clear water.

For the same reason spoons, unless they are small, are unsuitable baits under these conditions. They are too big and they tend to fish too deep unless fished very much faster than a spinner. And fishing too fast is one thing which must be avoided in dirty water. The salmon must have time to see the bait.

Summer spates pose special problems encountered only at this period of the season. In the earlier months of the year, rises in the river are caused by melting snow draining from the peaty uplands or by rain seeping through the surface of as yet unploughed and unworked agricultural land. Such spates are comparatively clear and, while they may colour the water to some degree, they contain little in the way of suspended impurities and in principle do not alter the pH value (the acidity) of the river appreciably.

In summer, matters are very different. The snow has gone.

Rain now drains off the surface and carries with it vast quantities of suspended matter from ploughed and harrowed fields, and this water, bearing much lime and phosphate in solution, is of a far higher pH value than that of the river. The effect on the fish is dramatic. Whereas a winter or early spring spate can merely be treated as a rise in the water level, that of a summer spate must be regarded as catastrophic for the angler.

It is unreasonable to suppose that salmon, who have neither the desire nor the necessity to feed, should respond to a stimulus which, under favourable circumstances, can occasionally awaken almost forgotten habits, when their normally clean habitat is suddenly transformed into the equivalent of the worst London fog.

Summer spates render the fish not only uncomfortable but probably desperately ill. Everything has gone wrong. The water they breathe has become alkaline rather than acid, it is full of suspended particles which settle on their delicate gill filaments, the light in their atmosphere dims and they are being constantly forced off their lies as the strength of the current increases. Is it any wonder that they are not interested in taking?

Yet the first minutes of a rise in the water are probably the most certain times for catching salmon that there are. As soon as they feel the water rising, hitherto dormant fish begin to be restless; and with disturbance start to move; and with movement then returns for a few moments the instinct of hunting. At such times everyone fishing on the beat hooks fish. But, depending on how quickly the river is rising, this magic is fleeting. It may last but a few minutes or extend to half an hour or more. But once over, the fisherman can put away his rods for the day. No fish will take until the water has stopped rising. Now, until the river starts to fall again there is a reasonable chance of catching the odd fish, close to the bank in slack areas or even in backwaters. But until the river has fallen back nearly to normal levels, until it runs clear and with little colour, fishing, be it with fly or bait, will offer few rewards.

There is an idea very prevalent among fly-fishermen that bait-fishing causes so much disturbance that it spoils the pool and puts the fish off from taking. This, of course, is nonsense. Properly fished and of the correct size, a small bait cast with a monofil nylon line across a pool causes far less disturbance than a fly cast with a thick plaited fly-line. And anyone who imagines that a 2in minnow swimming in a river full of trout, par and smolts is causing any unnatural disturbance must have a very strange idea of what life is like in the water world.

11

Prawn and Shrimp

The prawn as a bait can be deadly—deadly both in the sense that it can catch a lot of fish and also it can sometimes destroy a pool. It is a curious fact that at times salmon will almost fight to take a prawn, and at others are so scared of it that they can be seen literally jumping out of a pool in their haste to get away from it.

As with all forms of salmon fishing it is incumbent upon the fisherman to understand not only what he is doing and why, but also what the fish is doing and why he may be tempted by such a seemingly improbable lure.

Yet is it so improbable? We have all heard such remarks as, 'Salmon must be crazy to take a boiled prawn fished backwards!'. Such expressions give rise to the certainty that the fisherman who utters them is of the 'chuck and chance it' school and understands neither what he is trying to do nor to what stimuli the fish may react. Of course a prawn is fished backwards. The only way a prawn can swim is backwards. But why a bait of prawn, and why does the fish react to it in such opposite ways?

The salmon feeds at sea—and this is confirmed now that the drift-netsmen have discovered how to catch salmon in the open sea—in certain selected areas which all have one thing in common. They are where the warm currents flowing northwards meet the cold currents flowing south from under the polar ice. Here is a vast precipitation of salts, an inflorescence of diatom, here the sea is fluorescent with copepods and it is here that not only do the cod, the plaice, halibut, turbot and herring and most of the other species of cold-water fish derive their nourishment, but even the great blue whales. Some of these creatures, the salmon among them, will hunt smaller fish such as capelin, or young herring and spratts. Others such as the whalebone whales eat krill, small shrimps which exist in such numbers that it suffices for them merely to open their mouths to acquire a mouthful of food.

Basically the salmon appears to hunt small fish. In the Baltic, where for centuries the islanders of Bornholm have caught immature feeding salmon on set lines in the sea, the hooks are baited with herring, and it seems probable that this type of fish is the main prey of the salmon. But many of these fish are shoal fish, and as such are not always there since the shoals tend to break up and move away at certain seasons of the year. But always in these areas of the ocean are to be found two other types of creature which almost certainly form part of the salmon's diet. These are the prawns and shrimps, and squids and cuttlefish. And it would seem that when many of the ocean fish move away from their feeding grounds in the summer time to shallower coastal water where they breed, the pelagic salmon is left to find his sustenance from the shellfish and the squid family which remain. Prawns and shrimps may vary in colour from pale brown to bright vermilion, and loligo, the commonest family of the smaller squids, can be of almost any colour. It should be noted, too, that squid and cuttlefish also swim backwards.

The inference to be drawn from this potted piece of natural history is that the prawn is a summer bait. And this is found to be the case. It would be as complete a waste of effort to fish the prawn in February as to spin a sizeable sprat through a pool in June.

Prawn and Shrimp

Nowadays the most usual manner of fishing the prawn is on a spinning tackle. The most popular types have two sets of triangles, but equally effective is a single hook of about 9/0 size. Prawns, especially those preserved in bottles rather than fresh prawns kept in salt, tend to break up somewhat easily and need to be tied to the tackles with some care. They should be fished with a cast which must be well weighted as far away from the bait as is reasonable.

Spinning prawns should be fished slowly and, whereas it is most unusual for fish to follow a minnow when it is being wound in at the end of a cast, this is a common practice with the prawn. I once sat in a boat in the Home Catch Pool at Boughrood on the Wye and took six fish in a morning, all of which followed my prawn from a distance and practically jumped into the boat to take it at the last moment.

When really on the prawn, salmon seem to go mad for it. It is no unusual thing to see the bow waves of several fish coming from all directions to examine, even to fight for, the bait, and in a well stocked pool a fish is hooked literally at every cast.

But at other times not only will the prawn catch no fish but it will so scare them that they will even leave the pool altogether. I have a vivid memory of standing on the Glentanar bank of the Coble Pool on the Dee while a man on the Dinnet side fish a prawn. Every time the bait went into the water several fish jumped out obviously scared to death, and could be seen rushing out of the bottom of the pool.

What explanation can there be of such a phenomenon?

(*overleaf*) The Tay in its lower reaches is not everyone's idea of the perfect salmon river. It is too big to be waded save in low water and the streams often cannot be covered even from a boat when fly-casting. So harling is the time-honoured means of fishing. Very sociable, very comfortable, sometimes very cold, harling requires neither skill nor the expenditure of energy on the part of the angler. Today even the boatman does nothing except steer the boat to and fro across the stream while three rods each trail 30 yards of line behind the outboard motor. But a lot of fish are taken this way (*L. S. Paterson*)

125

That there is this duality in the reactions of salmon to the prawn is uncontested. All fishermen have noted it—but why?

We have mentioned the loligo, the small squid or cuttlefish which also swims backwards, and which, with its trailing tentacles and erratic movement, must look very similar to a swimming prawn. But whereas the crustacean depends on its shell for protection, the cuttlefish, squid and octopus have a far more effective insurance. They all exude a noxious inky fluid (from which the dye sepia used to be made) into the face of their pursuer. Can it be that under certain circumstances your prawn is mistaken for loligo? Is the fish frightened of a poisonous irritant about to be sprayed into his delicate gill membranes?

This is a possible explanation—and whether right or wrong does not really matter. But, if accepted, it at least serves to illuminate the one cardinal principle which applies to prawn-fishing. If in a stocked pool no fish takes or follows your bait in the first few casts, it is not only useless to continue, but you may very well destroy that pool for all forms of fishing for days afterwards.

BOBBING

In certain rivers, more especially those with rocky bottoms, a more effective way of fishing the prawn is by bobbing. Here the bait is set on a large, single hook and has no spinner. A spiral lead is set about a yard above it and, usually from a fly-rod with a reel fitted with a monofil nylon line, the bait is cast rather upstream and is allowed to bob down along the rock-ledges where the fish are lying.

To fish the bobbing prawn successfully—that is, without losing all the tackle—it is necessary to know the bottom of the pool in every detail and, for this reason, it is a method of fishing only suited to those who fish the same water year after year. It is a most amusing way of prawn-fishing and requires great skill and a delicate sense of touch. When the line comes to a standstill it is often difficult to discover whether it is a fish which has stopped the bait or if the lead is hung up on an obstacle. Sometimes the salmon will do no more than stop the prawn and hold it in his mouth until you pull; at other times he will seize it viciously and try to pull the rod out of your hands.

The bobbing prawn should always be fished with a loop of the line held in the fingers of your free hand. The sensitivity of your fingertips will, with practice, often be able to distinguish between a fish holding the bait and a rock snagging the lead.

In autumn and late summer the prawn is sometimes a very deadly bait, so deadly indeed that if persisted with, can over the space of a few days take virtually every fish, now red and full of roe, out of the pools. Whether these fish should be taken at all by any means of fishing is an arguable point. I personally think they should not even be fished for and, if caught, should certainly be returned to the river. But to set out with a prawn to kill as many as possible cannot be the aim of anyone who loves fishing as a sport.

Fishing a spinning shrimp bears about the same relationship to prawn-fishing as greased-line to sunk-line fly-fishing. Very light tackle, usually with single-handed rods, very little weight and small hooks are the requirements.

The spinning shrimp is merely the alternative to the greased-line fly or the small summer minnow. It must be fished near the surface, must be kept on the move and it must spin properly. I do not think that it is regarded by the salmon as a crustacean or a squid in the way that the prawn is seen, but merely as another small representation of whatever he might be feeding on in the sea at this time of year. On the whole it is not a very successful bait and does not compare for effectiveness with either the small fly or the minnow. But I suppose when all else fails it relieves the tedium to change one's bait—and miracles, happily, do happen.

Prawn and Shrimp

The bobbing shrimp, not often used and certainly a bait which is singularly unsuccessful in catching salmon (though trout, and especially sea trout, sometimes take it readily) is nothing other than a too-small prawn. It is most difficult to fish effectively since the amount of lead required to get this very light bait down to the rock-ledges is disproportionate to the size of the bait. As a result the shrimp cannot be made to look natural in any way.

Of recent years there has been much discussion about the ethics of prawn- and shrimp-fishing. The contras argue that these baits are unfair because, when the salmon are taking them they catch too many fish too easily, and when not taking them they frighten all the salmon and ruin the pool for other fishermen. The pros' argument is founded generally on the thesis that if you go fishing it is to catch fish and that if the prawn or shrimp is more successful than the fly or spinning bait, then you should use it. They assert, further, that if sometimes the prawn scares away the salmon or puts them off taking for a time, then someone else will benefit later on.

Both sets of argument are valid. It remains for the individual to decide for himself to which school of thought he subscribes. Whether you approve or disapprove of fishing with prawn and shrimp depends entirely on how you define the sport of fishing as against merely catching fish. Obviously if catching fish is your only objective, then your proper tools are a net, grappling hooks and leisters. If a fly-only man, then any other bait is not sporting. Somewhere between these two extremes must lie the decision which every fisherman must make for himself.

12

Fishing the Worm

Both the fly-fisherman and the bait-fisherman will affect to regard you as an outcast if you proudly announce that the only fish taken that day were the two you caught on a worm. Worm-fishing is still looked down upon on even second-rate salmon rivers, while the very mention of it in such exclusive circles as the Dee or Tweed angling fraternities is sufficient to brand the speaker as no gentleman.

Nevertheless, catching salmon with the worm is not only a great art but, given the proper conditions, an enthralling and rewarding form of fishing. Any fool can hook a salmon on a May morning in a well stocked pool with a small fly fished with a floating line. The veriest tyro cannot fail to catch fish harling the great pools of the lower Tay when the spring or autumn fish are running. If still able to lift a rod at all the most senior citizen can expect to average half a dozen fish a day on those deadly dull lochs of the Grimersta. But put any of these on a small river, dead low, on a sunny summer's day and they would hardly bother to fish even though the pools were teeming with salmon. Yet it is in such, otherwise hopeless, conditions that the art of worm-fishing is best practised. But we must deal first with the rather less artistic and inelegant means of catching salmon in a dirty spate river.

The pre-requisites under these circumstances are first, that

131

the water shall not be cold. It is seldom worthwhile attempting to use worms until the beginning of May, and certainly useless while there is any snow water coming down the river. Secondly, that the river shall be big and dirty. In very big spates fish desert the streams, now flowing much too fast for them, and tend to lie along the banks. As a general rule they avoid backwaters and will be found wherever the river flows gently close to the bank. Indeed, salmon very often lie in quite shallow water on the grassy banks from which the angler stands to cast when the river is at normal height. Thirdly, that the water shall be coloured and dirty. Summer spates, once the snow has gone and frost is out of the ground, are always dirty as most of the extra water derives from the farmed lowlands and the peat bogs of the uplands, now crumbling after the winter frosts.

In these dirty summer spates a lot of fish, both salmon and sea trout, can be caught on the worm. The method, requiring neither finesse nor art, makes little demand on either skill or imagination. It does not matter whether a fly-rod and line or a bait-rod is used. It is seldom necessary to fish the bait more than a few feet away.

The bait itself is unattractive. It consists of about half a dozen lob-worms threaded on to an 8/0 or 9/0 hook which is attached by a short nylon cast to the line. Since the fish will be lying in water moving very slowly and not more than a few feet in depth, only enough lead to take the bait down is necessary. In order to avoid snags it is better to spread this weight by means of split lead pellets or thin lead wire rather than a single spiral lead.

The bunch of worms is now cast a few feet into the stream, is allowed to swing round into the slacker water at its edge and as the bait is carried down the river the angler either lets out line from the reel or, more simply, walks down the bank with it.

I have seen a dozen sea trout and three or four salmon

taken from one small pool in the Spey in little more than an hour by this means. With strong tackle (and fine casts are quite unnecessary) the fish can be hauled ashore at once, and when on the take, which is usually at the height of the spate and for an hour or two afterwards, whoever is fishing with a bunch of worms cannot help but catch fish. But this is not salmon fishing.

Very different is worm-fishing in low, clear water under a strong summer sun. Whereas I do not care for spinning save in certain small rather special rivers, and have devoted perhaps too much of my life to fathoming the mysteries of my great love, fly-fishing, I have nevertheless derived immense pleasure and acquired much understanding of the behaviour of salmon from the many happy days I have spent fishing the worm in high summer.

Without doubt, the ideal rivers for worm-fishing are first, small rivers, and secondly, streams which do not have large populations of trout or coarse fish. These latter are a perfect nuisance to the worm-fisherman, as when feeding it is almost impossible to fish the bait to the salmon without their going for it. Consequently, it is the fast-flowing rivers of the North, which contain little weed or aqueous growth, are clear, and harbour few trout and no coarse fish save the summer run of eels, which are ideal. Such a river is the Aven or A'an, the main tributary of the Spey. Absolutely clear (every fish can be seen, with polarized glasses, lying in the pools), fast-flowing and with deep rocky pools connected to each other by shallows broken up by great stones which form little streams and pools in the shallows themselves, the Aven is perhaps the perfect river for summer, low water, worm-fishing.

The inexperienced who fish such a river for the first time will attempt to use a small spinning-rod and reel for worm-fishing. But this is not satisfactory. Essentially, this bait must be fished from a fly-rod, and a single-handed rod of at least 10ft in length.

133

Fishing the Worm

In the earlier weeks when the worm can first be successful, from about the last week in April to mid-May with the river not too low, the water still cool and the sun not too strong, it is the pools proper that are fished. The salmon are not yet lying in the strong, broken streams, and the sea trout have not yet run. The river, though still at a good fishing level, is quite clear and there is a tendency for the salmon to be running even at the height of the day.

Through his polarized glasses the fisherman can see that there are salmon lying in their accustomed lodges. Without disturbing them he retires from the bank and sets up his rod. Ideally, this is a rod of 10ft 6in to 11ft which is light enough to be used single-handed, yet powerful enough to give a measure of control when playing a heavy fish. Today it is probably true to say that a fibreglass rod is the most suitable since split cane rods are heavier and also become very liable to damage under the stress imposed not only in playing big fish but, above all, in releasing the inevitable snagged tackle. Greenheart rods cannot be recommended as they are either too whippy or too heavy, and will certainly be broken.

A fly-reel carrying a monofil nylon line with a breaking strain of about 12lb and with a large diameter drum is much easier to use than is a spinning-reel.

The tackle required is, first, a supply of good lob-worms. These can either be dug up and stored in moss to harden or, better still, picked up with the aid of a torch from a lawn at night. It is well worth ensuring that the worms are allowed to harden in clean moss, otherwise they will break up on the hooks and will frequently have to be replaced. Some people, I believe, keep them in sand and feed them by pouring a little milk into the sand-box. I have not been as successful in preserving worms in this manner. The best worms are from $2\frac{1}{2}$in to $3\frac{1}{2}$in long and neither too pale nor too dark.

Worm tackles, usually known as Stewart tackles, can be bought. But these are in no way as satisfactory as three No 8

134

eyed hooks tied at $\frac{1}{2}$–$\frac{3}{4}$in intervals on the cast knotted both at the eye and halfway down the shank.

The cast, which should be approximately 3ft in length and of a rather lower breaking strain than the monofil line, should be attached to a ball-bearing swivel which is at the end of the line. This swivel is most important since the shape adopted by the worm in the water invariably makes it spin in the current. Without a swivel the line very soon acquires a twist.

The amount of lead required is dependent on the speed of the current and the depth of the water in the chosen pool. As a general principle the less weight used the better. Any form of spiral of ball lead must be avoided. They always catch snags while fishing. Split lead shot, not too tightly pinched on to the cast so that they become detached if hung up, are much better. But best of all is fine lead wire wound into a spiral round a needle and threaded on to the cast about 1ft below the swivel.

The worm should be put head downwards on all three hooks with a few millimetres at each end of the worm being free. Rolling the worm in clean sand makes it far easier to hold while putting it on to the hooks.

Worm-fishing under such conditions is often known as up-stream worm-fishing, and from this description it might be thought that the angler started at the bottom end of the pool and worked his way up as in dry-fly trout fishing; such is not the case. The reason this is called upstream fishing is that in order to get the bait to sink before reaching the fish, it is cast upstream and allowed to be carried to the bottom as it moves unchecked downstream.

In the ordinary way the fisherman starts at the head of the pool and casts, underhand as if bowling, his worm into the rough water at the neck of the pool. As the worm is carried down past him, the angler strips line off the reel and, maintaining the very minimum of tension with his fingers, allows the worm to fish down the pool and swing gradually into his

own bank. The cast is then recovered by hauling in the line and coiling it in big coils either on the bank or held in the hand. The upstream cast is now repeated when the angler has moved a yard or two down the pool.

Casting the worm is not as easy as it sounds. It has to be done underhand and with a steady swing of the rod. Any jerk such as is used in fly-casting will send the worm flying off the hooks, so practice is necessary. Those who have mastered the technique can cast a worm, virtually without lead, almost as far across the stream as they can place a fly and can, as a result, present their bait to every fish in the pool.

Armed with the correct tackle and with the ability to cast the worm, the fisherman must learn how to fish this bait. The first thing to understand is that no salmon ever takes anything which is actually on the bottom and below his own level. This is why the lead is placed 2ft or so above the worm hooks. Though the lead may hit the bottom, the worm should not and it is not fishing if it does.

As the cast moves downstream the lead will be felt by the fingers on the line occasionally to touch a rock or a stone. Sometimes, too, it will lodge in a crevice. But while it keeps moving it must be allowed to swim down the river unchecked. Sometimes it will go 40–50yd before either checking or drifting into slack water beside the bank. In this event some of the line should be reeled back before the last 15yd or so are left to be coiled.

Whenever the line is felt to check, a very slight tension must be put on it with the fingers. If it remains motionless, it is probable that either the lead or the bait is caught up, when a

The Tweed at Kelso is another big river and has largely to be fished from a boat. Our angler here is fishing the fly—probably greased line as it is a warm day in late spring. The boatman is pulling just enough to allow the boat to drift slowly downstream. But I think the angler is not too hopeful, content to sit comfortably smoking his pipe while his cast is fishing itself out (*Charles Grant*) sharp pull will often release it. A fish, however, betrays him-self almost at once by giving sharp little pulls as he nibbles at the worm. Trout give very fast but often quite heavy pulls and can, with experience, usually be recognized. Unless you want to catch small trout it is best to pull the bait away from them as soon as possible.

Salmon, however, while often doing little more than stop-ping the worm, will eventually start to give quite solid slow pulls on the line. The action called for from the fisherman is simple. Do absolutely nothing. You can now, if you wish, light a cigarette, sit down, or even put your rod down. But do not strike and do not pull. Eventually, it may often be as long as a full minute—and a minute can seem an awful long time under such circumstances—the line will be seen to move away. The fish has taken the bait and is moving away with it as he feels the hooks. Now you may tighten up in the com-plete certainty that you have hooked the fish.

On occasion, especially when fish are lying in very fast streams, they will take with a bang and rush off with the bait at once. They are usually well hooked when they do this. Sea trout, particularly, often take the worm in this manner.

There is a widely held belief that salmon which take the worm do not play well. Let no one persuade you of this. In my experience the best playing fish of all are those caught on the worm in low, clear and warm water. In small rivers you will be lucky if able to land them in the pool in which they have been hooked, and may indeed be faced with running at full speed either up or downstream (in low water a lot of fish leave a pool for the shallows above it) in order to main-tain contact.

When fishing a pool with the worm it must be remembered that very often you can see the fish—and that, therefore, they can see you. Fortunately salmon, but not trout and sea trout, very soon forget any alarm you may have caused when moving into your stance on the bank. At first they will all move away.

But if you stand still for a few minutes they can be observed moving back into the erstwhile lies. You have now become part of the landscape and when you wave your rod about directly over them will take no notice of you as you stand fishing.

In high summer when the water is very low and warm, fishing the pools with the worm will probably be no more rewarding than with fly or spinning bait. Occasionally, salmon will take in the white water of the strong streams at the head of the pool and it is usually worthwhile swimming the worm down the top few yards of pools with strong streams of broken water at their head. But, in general, it will be in the rocky shallows where the water, even in the holes behind the bigger boulders, seldom attains a depth of 3ft, that a lot of salmon hide themselves. Those whose fishing is confined to fly-fishing or bait-fishing in our better known salmon rivers seldom realize that when the river drops to summer level, when the water warms up and when the hot sun of mid-summer drives off much of the available oxygen from the river water, a great number of salmon leave the pools and find themselves lies in little holes and streams in the shallows. When the river rises again these fish return to the pools and often give rise to the assumption that they are either an autumn run or have moved upstream from the lower reaches.

No greater pleasure can be experienced than, on a hot summer's day, with thigh waders, a fly-rod, polarized glasses and a plentiful supply of lob-worms and tackles, to take to the river at the top of the beat and wade one's way downstream fishing all the deeper runs and holes in the shallows between the pools. Great accuracy in casting is needed, for the worm must be allowed to fish behind every rock. Virtually no lead at all must be used and great care must be taken to see that the tackle is not snagged.

If there is a run of sea trout in the beat it is almost inevitable that a few will be hooked—and great fun they are. But a salmon hooked here is something to dream about. He is in shallow water and nothing makes a salmon more anxious and, consequently, more active, than finding himself in danger of stranding. He will make for the nearest pool either upstream or downstream. The problem for the angler is how to prevent his line being caught up behind or under a rock. Very often the line will be seen pointing in one direction when a fish—your fish—will jump out of the water in a totally different place.

Between wading across to free a line snagged behind a rock, splashing up or downstream in water of varying depths, running at times to try to recover some of the line, pausing to try to find out where the fish is and eventually following him into a pool and landing him, you will have had all the excitement of a dozen or more fish caught and landed in a pool.

In very hot weather and very low water, salmon will not take a big lob-worm even in broken white water. But they can be caught with very small worms fished on tackles made up of two, rather than three hooks, and of sizes as small as No 10 and on very fine nylon casts. Obviously the combination of fine casts and the additional hazards of extremely low water greatly increase the dangers of breaking and a number of fish will inevitably be lost in this way. To many of us there is a distaste occasioned by the thought of a salmon breaking and swimming away with a set of worm hooks in its mouth and gullet. Yet, though in rivers where worm-fishing is a prevalent practice there must be many dozens of such cases in a season, it is virtually unknown to find a fish dead for such a reason.

Of course, worm-fishing is a deadly method of catching salmon in big, well stocked rivers as well as in little rivers. In Iceland, for instance, the locals confine their fishing to the worm, fished on a big single hook and a very strong cast. They are only interested in catching fish—not in fishing. In these beautiful fly pools, an Icelander will happily haul out thirty fish a day on the worm which is taken very readily by fresh-run fish.

Monofil nylon lines are sometimes tricky to handle. If kept wound tightly on a small diameter reel they coil them-selves up like clock-springs when stripped off and laid on the ground beside the fisherman. Life is made much easier for the angler if a large diameter reel is used and if, as the line is stripped off the reel, it is then straightened by pulling it firmly before laying it down.

A final word about worm-fishing. This is not to be recom-mended as a standard method of fishing good fly-rivers when there is a reasonable chance of catching salmon by normal means. Indeed, unless it is desperately required to catch a fish when all other methods have failed, the worm is not much fun to fish in any pool of a fair-sized river. In a river full of small trout or of eels, fishing this bait in the pools is a most frustrating experience. The worm never has time to be seen by a salmon but is always being nibbled at by one of these species. If the angler has the misfortune to hook an eel it is a virtual impossibility either to kill the fish or remove the hooks, and he will end up with hands and line covered in thick slime.

But in dead low water in our smaller salmon rivers, you can have a lot of fun fishing the worm. Even on a hot bright afternoon when all other ways of fishing are hopeless, you can still catch a salmon or a sea trout with the worm. Even in big rivers like the Spey or Dee, a hot July afternoon spent fishing the runs in the shallows between the pools can be most amusing and often very rewarding.

13

Dry-Fly Fishing and Float-Fishing

One of the outstanding mysteries of the art of salmon fishing lies in the diversity of the behaviour of the fish towards the dry fly in different parts of the world. In the USA and Canada, for instance, it is a standard method of fishing to use a large hairy 'bumble' type of fly fished dry with a floating line. The fish rise to, and take, these lures very readily. In Norway, when fishing in bright sunlight with a dry fly for sea trout, which can only virtually be caught in daylight by this means, it is not uncommon to rise several salmon and to hook the occasional fish. Yet, though many fishermen have experimented with the dry fly on British rivers the results have been, almost without exception, a complete failure.

I have tried the dry fly, American and Canadian patterns many times. Under normal good fishing conditions, when the river has been running at normal heights and the water and air temperature have been normal for the time of year, the results have been pathetic, and not a single fish has evinced the slightest interest in the fly. This has applied both to the early spring, in sunk-fly conditions, and to late spring and summer in greased-line conditions.

The Aven below Tormintoul. This delightful little river is the main tributary of the Spey. Fast flowing and clear it fills with fish from April onwards. Fast streams are ideal for upstream worm-fishing or fly-fishing (*C. A. Peto*)

Nevertheless, under certain circumstances, very often those considered the most adverse, a reaction, an activity, which gives rise to hope can be induced in the salmon with the dry fly.

A few seasons ago when fishing the Spey in July with the river running 1ft below normal and in bright hot weather I tried out the dry fly. My friend, Lester Ruwe, a most skilful and experienced salmon fisherman, had left me a few of his American flies. What their names were I had no idea. They were monstrosities, some black, some brown, some red with coloured hackles, and all were about as big as a 6/0 fly tied so that it was more than half as broad as it was long.

The first problem which confronted me was how to fish it properly. Obviously, it had to be fished upstream, and this meant starting at the bottom of the pool and wading upstream. This may be easy in the slow-running trout streams of the south, but it is a formidable task in a river like the Spey. I found, however, a pool with a narrow stream and fairly slack water at the side up which I could wade without too much difficulty. There were a few fish in the stream and there was no problem in reaching them and in fishing the fly over them in a reasonable dry-fly manner.

The next problem was that of the type of rod and size of line which should be used. Obviously, a big fuzzy fly created much air resistance when being cast, and therefore needed a fairly heavy line to carry it. This meant a powerful rod. Les Ruwe, when demonstrating his method the previous year, had used a very stiff little rod of no more than 8ft carrying a rather heavy line. No doubt this was perfectly adequate in rivers on the American continent when fishing from a canoe. But it was hopelessly inadequate in a large wading river. It was possible, using maximum effort to get the distance required, but virtually impossible to fish the fly or control the line once it had been cast. So I used a 12ft 6in rod with a greased No 6 Kingfisher line. This was entirely satisfactory.

I had noted that very long (about 15ft) casts were used, and I presumed that these were necessary to keep the fly well away from the floating line. I tied on a brown 'monstrosity' and cast it into the stream. Almost immediately a fish made a beautiful head and tail rise at it. But it never touched the fly. I tried again, and again, and again. Always I got fish to rise, never did I get a fish to take. They came up right at the fly, sometimes with their mouths open, sometimes closed. Sometimes they 'boiled' at it, at other times they came half out of the water to it. But they were always 1–2in short of the fly. And as long as I was prepared to go on fishing on that bright hopeless afternoon, so long were the fish prepared to rise at, but never take, my fly.

I have tried since many times, and in every case the story has been the same. In normal, good fishing conditions, it is rare that any salmon looks at the dry fly in our rivers. But in very low water, in very warm weather and in the most adverse conditions of sun and sky, they can be induced to a degree of activity seldom ever seen at other times.

We may well ask ourselves how it comes about that the same fish, the Atlantic salmon, which in every other respect behaves in exactly the same manner in America, in Scandinavia, in Europe and in Britain can apparently behave so differently when it comes to its reactions to the dry fly. But when we look a little more closely at the problem we begin to see that the circumstances are not identical in Britain with those in other localities.

First, the seasons are different. In these islands we have a climate which is totally different from the continental type of climate of North America and Europe. We do not normally have winters of such low temperatures that a high proportion of our rivers, or at any rate, the higher reaches of them, are frozen over. We have high waters throughout the winter. Continental climates mean very low rivers during the freeze-up of winter. We do not have to await the thaw for our rivers to

145

rise and allow the fish to run. In short, those fish in our main salmon rivers can and do run throughout the year. Indeed, it is said that there is no day in the whole year on which some fish do not attempt to enter the Spey or the Irish Blackwater.

The main runs in the Irish and the Scottish East Coast rivers are late winter and early spring runs, when the water is cold and the sun is low. But in places where continental climate conditions prevail, the main, indeed the only runs, occur during summer when, even though it is melting ice and snow which swells the river, the water is quickly warmed in the summer sun.

When examining the circumstances under which salmon are caught with the dry fly in America it is clear that two preconditions are necessary. The first is that only fresh-run fish can be caught, and the second, that the water temperature must be at least 70°F.

Such conditions do not, save in the most exceptional circumstances, exist in Britain. The only times when the water temperatures in our rivers rise to 70°F or above are in high summer under drought conditions. At such times it becomes impossible for fresh fish to run into our rivers. Occasionally, however, we do get a run of grilse and of small summer salmon in the month of July which enter when the river is very warm and very low. But, by and large, nobody dreams of fishing during the heat of the day while the sun it at its height. And it is at such times, judging from American experience, that success with the dry fly might be achieved. If I am lucky enough to encounter such conditions again, I propose to give the dry fly an extended trial, for I do not believe that fish which show so much interest in this here cannot be caught with the dry fly.

In the last few years a method of fly-fishing which does not require the ability to cast with a fly-rod, nor even the use of one, has become popular. This is, in fact, nothing other than bait-fishing with light tackle, but using a fly as a lure rather than a bait.

The method is simple. You cannot cast a fly with a spinning-rod because it is too light. If you put on such a lead as is necessary to allow you to cast, it fishes the fly too deep, so a weight which does not sink, which does not show up when floating, or when submerged, yet is heavy enough to cast, is required. To this semi-submersible weight is attached the fly on a longish nylon or gut cast.

This weight is nothing other than a plastic sphere or bubble, colourless and transparent like glass and about $1\frac{1}{2}$in in diameter. This is filled with water and, when cast from a spinning-rod, carries the fly out and allows it to be fished as if it were a bait. The bubble can be floated or fished submerged at will. The degree to which it is filled with water determines this. When submerged it is invisible in the water. When floating it may create 'bow waves' as it fishes, but is otherwise practically invisible to the fish.

I would not claim that bubble-fishing is either elegant or competitive with proper fly-fishing under normal circumstances. Yet there are situations in which it can be most useful and indeed sometimes the only way of fishing a fly, the small fly especially, with any chance of success.

The art of bubble-fishing lies in maintaining such control of the bubble, and therefore of the fly, that it never fishes too fast, seldom drags and is kept moving with a water speed which is reasonable and akin to that of the creature which the fly represents. In other words it must be fished like a fly and not like a bait.

As the most successful bubble-fishing is concerned with the small fly—there is no advantage in using it with the sunk fly as the spinning baits are really more practical—the equipment required is that for summer bait-fishing. A small rod, a fixed spool or multiplying revolving drum reel, a fine nylon monofil or plaited line and a bubble. For those who have not

147

tried this method of fishing it is well worth the small outlay required for the sake of experimenting with it. And not only will much pleasure be derived, but often fish will be caught with the bubble which could be taken in no other way.

14

Fair Fishing

The ethics of salmon fishing are essentially personal. *Quot homines tot sententiae.* What is right for one man is often wrong for another. The foul-hooked fish and what to do about him is a case in point.

Inevitably in a lifetime a number of fish will be foul-hooked. The law is quite specific about it. They should be returned to the water. But, in my experience, a fisherman who inadvertently hooked a salmon by the back fin and landed him would be considered to have lost his reason if he returned the fish to the river. Indeed, for many, the highlights of the past concern epic struggles with fish hooked in the tail or fin, played for hours and landed miles downstream.

The foul-hooked salmon is invariably a monster fish if he is lost. If landed, it is with astonishment that he is usually found to be nothing out of the ordinary. Yet curiously enough the biggest salmon I have caught in Britain was foul-hooked in the tail with a No 6 Logie in the Dog Pool of the Inverness-shire Garry. He took me rather under a mile downstream and

(*overleaf*) The Aven; in June, when the big sea trout shoals run the Spey (which, by the way, is certainly the best sea trout river in Britain) this stream is virtually certain to yield a few fish of good size. Few realize that the average weight of the Spey system sea trout is about three pounds (*A. D. S. MacPherson*)

my gillie had to lift him out by the gills as he lay, half dead, head downstream, alongside one of the little jetties in the Long Pool. Needless to say, Dougal had left his net at the Dog Pool! The fish weighted 38lb.

That when fishing fair with fly or bait an occasional salmon will be foul-hooked is unavoidable, and the extra thrill experienced in playing and landing such fish can be regarded as the spice on the gingerbread of salmon fishing. But where does the dividing line between fishing fair and fishing foul lie?

As a young man I was privileged for many years to be invited by the late Randall Nicol to fish in February at Ballogie on the Dee. We fished only fly and, of course, big flies with 14–15ft rods and heavy lines. Spinning was considered, if not foul fishing, certainly unsporting. Four or five of us normally caught between seventy and ninety fish in the fortnight. To an onlooker nothing could have appeared more correct than the way we fished. Yet more than half of all the fish we caught were foul-hooked, and while no one would admit it, were snatched quite deliberately. In the Potarch Bridge Pool for instance, when the fish were there, or were running, you had only to stand and cast somewhat more square than normal with a long line over the last few yards of the pool and you were bound to hook a fish. If having had a blank day on some other pools, it was quite normal to be invited to have a few casts in the Bridge Pool before packing up. And to those of us who knew what we were doing this seldom failed.

There is a general belief that it is easier to foul-hook fish with a bait than with a fly. This is a fallacy. The only man I have ever seen who could regularly foul-hook with a bait was Donald Grant, the gillie-fisherman employed by the Mugiemoss Paper Mills to fish the famous Saugh Pool in the Don. He used to catch 100 plus every spring to his own rod out of this pool—and if the fish did not take he used to foul-hook them in the tail of the pool with a sand-eel exactly weighted for the height of the water and cast to within a few inches of a lie favoured by every fish entering the pool.

These examples of catching salmon by unethical or illegal means may be amusing, but are not to be condoned. The essence of true angling is that the fisherman does not catch a fish. The fish catches a fisherman. But alas, with salmon daily becoming more valuable, with rents forever rising, with more and more fishermen competing for fewer and fewer fish, all sorts of practices which would certainly have been considered unethical a generation past are now commonplace. We used always to stop fishing, save for a summer evening for grilse or sea trout, on the lower and middle beats of the Dee at the end of May. There were no more runs of fresh fish and we did not fish for stale red salmon.

Today, more fish, all of them gravid, red or black, are killed in September than in any other month. In one of the tributaries of the Spey I have seen a party of sportsmen arrive for the last fortnight of the season's fishing with a portable refrigerator towed behind their car. Fishing with big worm tackles in a dead low river full of fish, it was a poor day that they did not take out twenty fish, not one of them taken by the mouth.

Let me end this book as I began it. Catching salmon is a misnomer. The angler does not seek to catch his quarry. The essence of fishing as a sport is that the fisherman deliberately denies himself any and every means of trapping, snaring or netting an unwilling prey into his basket. He sets himself a set of rules which effectively denies him the right to catch a fish and which ensures that success can be arrived at only when the fish catches the angler. The moment there is any deviation from this basic principle then the angler is not fishing—he is poaching.

Index

Page numbers in italic indicate illustrations

agents, of fishing rights, 50
amusement, and fish taking, 12
anger, and fish taking, 9–10, 19
angle of casting, 114–15
Angler's Creel, 9
Aven (A'An), river, 118, 133, *143*, *150–1*

bait, 62;
  why salmon takes, 7–12, 20–2, 24, 35–7
bait fishing, 105–25, 128–35, 137–41, 147
Bann, river, 79
beat, choice of, 50–2
bed of river, effect of, 28, 70–1
best time to fish, 37, 38, 51
Blackwater (Irish), *43*, *48–9*, 79, *101*, 146
Blue Charm, 78, 80
bobbing, 128–30
bottom fishing, 107, 128–35, 137–41
Bridge Pool, Potarch, 39, 152
bubble-fishing, 147–8

Cairnton, 83
Calderwood, Mr, 27
capelin, 13, 15, 21
carborundum stone, 47
cast:
  cleaning, 79
  greased-line, 79
  nylon, 79, 140
  prawn and shrimp, 125
  sunk-fly, 46

  worm fishing, 135
casting, *32*, *43*, *57*;
  greased-line, 90–8, 100, 102–5
  prawn and shrimp, 125, 128
  spinning, 114–16, 118–22
  sunk-fly, 56, 58–9, 65–71
cold, sensitivity to, 26–37
colour of fly, 59–63, 77–8
Cooper, John Ashley, *101*
costs, 51–2, 53
curiosity, and fish taking, 10–11, 19
current speed, river:
  and fish running, 28
  effect on speed of fly, 93–4, 97–8
  effect on type of fly, 86–8, 89
  swimming speed needed, 37–9
current, warm sea, 19, 21, 22
cuttlefish, 21, 124, 127

Days and Nights of Salmon Fishing in the Tweed, 12
Dee (Aberdeenshire), *14*, 38, 39, *115*, 125, 141;
  ethics of fishing in, 152
  gut to use, 79
  numbers caught in, 51, 108
  size of rod used, 110, 152
  winter water level, 70
Devon bait, 111, 112
Devonshire, Duke and Duchess of, *43*, *48–9*
distance swum by running fish, 37–41

Index

dry-fly fishing, 142, 144–6
duality of life, sea/river, 17–22, 24, 28–9

egg laying, oxygen needed, 28–31
elver (*Leptocephalus*), 21, 84, 87
energy, conservation of, 35, 38, 38–9, 95
ethics, fishing, 108, 129, 130, 149, 152–3
eyes, 22, 26, 54–6, 58–63, 113

fasting, fresh water, 17–18
fear, reason for fish taking, 9, 19
feeding experiment, salmon fry, 76
feeding, at sea, 13, 15, 17, 21–2, 123–4
fibreglass rod, 134
flashing of bait, reason for fish taking, 10–11
float-fishing, 147–8
fly, dry, 142, 144–8
fly, greased-line fishing:
  choosing, 72, 75–8, 80–3
  colour important, 77–8
  presentation, 83–4, 86–91, 93–8, 100, 102–5
  size, 77
fly, sunk-line fishing:
  appearance to fish, 54–6, 58–9
  colour and tone, 59–63
  direction of, 66–70, *67*, *68*
  representing a fish, 62, 63–4, *61*, *63*
  speed of, 65–6, *65*
fly, why salmon takes, 7–12, 20–2, 24, 35–7
  fundamental requirement of, 62
  representing fish, 63
foul-hooked fish, 149, 152–3
fresh water, as habitat, 24–6
freshwater fish, salmon as, 15–16, 18
fry, feeding experiment, 76

gaff, *49*, 50, *101*, 105
Garry, river, Inverness, *69*, 149
Garry Dog, 112
gear:
  greased-line, 73–5
  summer spinning, 119–20
  sunk-line, 44–7, 50
  worm fishing, 133, 134–5
Glentanar, Deeside, 39, 125
Grant, Donald, 152
greased-line fishing, 72–84, *74*, 90–1, 93–8, 100, 102–5, 142
  choice of cast, 79
  choice of fly, 75–8, 80–2
Grey Mare pool, Blackhall, 39

habit, reason for fish taking, 19–22
hackles, 61
harling, *126–7*
hearing, sense of, 26
heat, sensitivity to, 26, 27
herring, as salmon food, 13, 15, 21
horizontal axis of fly, 69–70, 88, 89
hunger, 8, 9, 18

Iceland, worm fishing in, 140–1
instinct, and fish taking, 11–12, 19, 30
Inver, river, Sutherland, *99*

June, fishing in, 38

kelts, 9
Kingfisher No 5 rod, 73, *74*, 144
krill, 13, 21

large fly or bait season, 43
Lawson Pool, river Drum, 39
Laxford, river, *23*
Lebistes, swimming speed, 87
Leptocephalus, 21, 84, 87
life history of salmon, 13ff
line driers, 50

Index

lines
  bobbing, 128–9
  greased-line, 73–5
  monofil nylon, 109, 114, 115,
    122, 134, 141
  spinning, 109, 115–16
  sunk-line, 45–6
  worm fishing, 134, 137–8, 141
Lochy, river, *74*
Logie, fly, 78
loligo, 13, 15, 124, 128
long shank, low-water dressing,
  77, 88–9

MacNiven, Duncan, 118
Malloch, reel, 109, 114
May, as fishing month, 37, 38, 51
mending, 96–8
Menzies, W. J. M., 28, 34
migration, 13ff
minnows, as bait, 111, 116, 129

netting experiments, 25
Nicol Randall, 152
North America, 142, 144, 145, 146
nylon casts, 79, 140
nylon lines, 109, 114, 115, 122,
  134, 141

Oglesby, Arthur, *115*
over-fishing, 13
oxygen level:
  controlling whole behaviour,
    28–36, 41
  for egg laying and embryo,
    28–31
  insufficient in sea, 29
  need for fish to conserve, 95
  in polluted water, 31–2
  in pure water, 33–4
  reason for fish taking, 35–7
  variability in rivers, 26, 41, 139

Park on Dee, 38
physical change sea/river, 24–6,

17–18
plaited line, *48*, 114, 115
'pointing' the sunk fly, 66–9, *67*,
  68
polarized glasses, 47, 75
pollution, 31–3
pools, 35–6
  running salmon in, 39–41
  where salmon lie in, 39, 70–1,
    97, 113
Potarch Bridge Pool, 39, 152
prawns:
  sea food of salmon, fishing
    with, 123–5, 128–30
presentation of fly:
  dry-fly fishing, 144–8
  greased-line, 83–4, 86–9, 90–8,
    100, 102
  sunk-fly, 54–6, 58–71, *67*, *68*

rainfall, effect on river, 120–2,
  131–2
reel:
  float-fishing, 147
  greased-line, 75
  spinning, 109, 114–15, 119
  sunk-line, 45
  worm fishing, 134
reflecting properties of water,
  54–6, 58–9
refraction of light, 54, 55
reproduction, oxygen needed for,
  29, 30–2
respiration, 31, 34–5, 37
resting salmon, 38–41
rise, not necessary to see, 98, 100,
  102
riverbed, influence on running, 28
river level, influence on fish running, 41
rod:
  dry-fly, 144
  float fishing, 147
  greased-line, 72, 73–5
  spinning, *48*, 109–10

157

Index

sunk-line, 44–5, 45–6
worm fishing, 133, 134
Rosher, J. B., 82
running fish, 37–41
Ruwe, Lester, 144

salinity sea/fresh water, 25, 26
Salmo genus, 15–16
Salmon Fishing, 93
Salmon Fishing, Philosophy and Practice, 100
salmon fly, 54, 62, 63, *see also* fly
salmon fry feeding experiment, 76
Scandinavia, dry-fly in, 142, 145
scale markings, 13, 15, 22
schools of salmon, 39–40
scissors, 47
Scrope, William, 12
sea lice on salmon, 25
sea salmon:
  change in fresh water, 15–22, 24ff
  teeth, 9, 13
sea trout, *23, 150–1*
  dry-fly fishing, 142
  worm fishing, 132, 139, 141
sea water:
  lack of oxygen in, 29
  difference from fresh water, 25–6
senses of fishes, 26
September as fishing month, 51, 153
sexual glands and migration, 17
Shannon, river, 79, *85, 92*
Shin, river, Sutherland, *57*
shrimps, 129, 130
sight, 22, 26, 54–6, 58–63, 113
silex reel, 114–15
silk thread line, *48,* 114, 115
Silver-Blue, 78
spate conditions, *115,* 120–2, 131–3
specific gravity salt/fresh water, 25

Spey, river, 52, 70, 79, 109, 141, *143, 150–1,* 153
spinning, *48,* 109–22;
  angle of casting, 114–15
  depth of fishing, 112–14
  prawns, 125
  spoons, 116, 120
  type of bait, 110–12, 115–16
  unsporting, 152
spoons, 116, 120
spratts, 111, 112, 116, 124
spring rivers, reason for, 27–8
squid, 21, 124, 127
striking, 103–4, 118–19
summer rivers, reason for, 27–8
sunk-line fishing, 42–7, 50–6, 58–71, 142
  choice of fly, 53–4
  colour and tone of fly, 59–63
  fly representing fish, *61, 63,* 63–4
  gear, 44–7, 50
  period of, 42–3
  presentation, 54–6, 58–9, 65–70, *67,* 68
  weight of fly, 70–1
  when to use, 94, 95, 98, 107
  where to fish, 50–2
swimming distance, running fish, 37–9
swimming speed, running fish, 37–8

taking fly, 58, 100, 102–3, *103,* 138;
  reason for, 7–12, 20–2, 24, 35–7
Taverner, Eric, 10
Tay, river, 25, *32,* 109, *126–7*
Tchernavin, Dr, 9
teeth, 9, 13
temperature of water:
  deciding method of fishing, 42–3, 72, 94, 96
  effect of fish behaviour, 26–8, 42–3, 72, 76, 86, 94–5

158

and size of fly, 81, 82–3, 84, 86
variability in river, 26
thermometer, 50, 75, 81, 92–3, 96
Thomson, J. Arthur, 16
thunder and lightning, 78
tone and colour;
  bait, 112
  flies, 60–3, 77–8
touch, sense of, 26
trout, 15–16, 25;
  nuisance when worm fishing, 133, 141
  oxygen needs, 29, 29–30
  taking fly, moment of, 100, 138

trout rod, suitability of, 74–5
Tweed, river, *136*

waders, best type of, 47
wading stick, 50
Wandless, Mr, 9
water level, influence on fish, 41, 120–2, 131–2
water surface, seasonal importance of, 22
Wood, Arthur, 73–4, 78, 80, 83–4, 91
worm fishing, 107, 130–5, 137–41
  equipment, 133–5
  method, 135, 137–41